Childminder's Guide
to Child Development

Childminder's Guide to Child Development

Allison Lee

continuum

Continuum International Publishing Group

The Tower Building   80 Maiden Lane, Suite 704
11 York Road   New York
London SE1 7NX   NY 10038

www.continuumbooks.com

British Library Cataloguing-in-Publication Data
A catalogue record for this book is available from the British Library.

ISBN: 9781847060853 (paperback)

Library of Congress Cataloging-in-Publication Data
Lee, Allison.
Childminder's guide to child development/Allison Lee.
    p. cm.
    Includes index.
    ISBN-13: 978-1-84706-085-3 (pbk.)
    ISBN-10: 1-84706-085-4 (pbk.)
1. Child care workers – Training of. 2. Child care workers – Certification.
3. Child care workers – Employment. 4. Child development. 5. Early
childhood education – Activity programs. 6. Creative activities and seat
work. 7. Early childhood education – Parent participation. I. Title.

    HQ778.5.L438 2008
    305.23102′43627–dc22   2008017978

Typeset by Newgen Imaging Systems Pvt Ltd, Chennai, India
Printed and bound in Great Britain by Cromwell Press

Contents

Acknowledgements

My special thanks go to the parents of the children I have had the pleasure in working with both past and present. The duties I perform as a childminder, on a daily basis, have given me invaluable knowledge and hands-on experience in child development which has been beneficial to me when writing this book.

Thanks also go to my family for their continued encouragement and support.

Introduction

Learning about child development involves the study of patterns of growth and achievements, from which guidelines are drawn up to effectively cover the 'normal' milestones each child should achieve. However, it is essential that practitioners understand that these 'normative indicators' are precisely that; indicators of the general trends in development in children across the globe. It is vital that we look at each child as a 'whole' person, that is, take into account their *holistic development*. In order to get a true picture of a child's overall development we need to look at their development in terms of physical, emotional, intellectual, social, moral, spiritual and cultural aspects.

It is paramount that practitioners, while recognizing the milestones in a child's development, do not lose sight of how a child grows and develops as an *individual*. Although development is often approached in separate areas when making assessments it is important to remember that all aspects are related and they overlap and affect one another. For example a child with a hearing impairment or speech delay may have difficulty communicating with others which in turn may lead to a delay in interacting and forging friendships with their peers. This may lead to them becoming quiet and reserved or ultimately lead to anger and frustration.

Children grow and develop at differing speeds however, what is certain is that each stage of development follows on from the next. For example one child may learn to walk at the age of 10 months while another may be nearer to their second birthday before they have mastered the art however, both children will learn the task in the same stages; they will learn to sit before they stand, stand before they walk and walk before they run. Likewise speech can progress at varying rates and while some children cheerfully babble all day long others are much more likely to play in silence. What is important is that childminders understand that a child will progress through similar stages before mastering the task of communication for example they will go from making sounds, to forming words which will in turn lead to sentences after which the use of tenses will develop.

This book is intended as a guide for childminders and will help you to understand how a child develops. It will look at factors which influence child development and will encourage you to look at all aspects of a child's development and how you can help them to get the most out of the activities and resources you provide.

Understanding Child Development from Birth to 16 Years

This chapter directly relates to

- Unit 2 of the Diploma in Home-based Childcare: Childcare and Child Development (0–16) in the Home-based Setting
- The Learning and Development Requirements of The Early Years Foundation Stage

Before starting to understand how a child develops it is important to remember that all children, even tiny babies, are complex human beings and their development should be viewed, not in stages, but *holistically* that is as a whole. We need to take into account their physical, intellectual, language, emotional and social development rather than to simply focus on whether they can walk and talk at a certain stage of their development. Much emphasis is put on whether a child can walk at 12 months, talk at 18 months and control their bowel movements somewhere in between, however these are neither fair nor accurate assumptions on which to base our knowledge and understanding of child development. Although it is necessary to use developmental 'norms' often known as *milestones* when recognizing a child's stage of development, understanding child development is much more complex than simply looking at a chart showing milestones and comparing them to each individual child. Although these milestones are a useful *guideline* for helping to study the patterns of growth and development it must never be forgotten that a child's *holistic* development is what should be at the forefront of our minds at all times.

Because it is impossible to describe the development of each and every individual child this book will use the guidelines for 'normal' development and will show what *most* children should be expected to do at particular stages of their development.

Birth to 11 months

New-born babies rely heavily on their senses to explore their environment. Although their vision is not perfect they can focus on objects less than a metre away. Having emerged from their mother's womb they are now beginning to get used to a new and alien environment involving taste, smell, touch, light and noise.

At birth babies display a number of *primitive reflexes*. These are automatic movements which are inborn and are important indicators of the health of the babies' central nervous system. These primitive reflexes include:

- **The startle reflex** – sudden loud noises or bright lights will startle a new-born baby and they will involuntarily move their arms outwards.
- **The walking reflex** – if a new-born baby is gently held upright with their feet on a firm surface they will make forward stepping movements which resemble walking.
- **The rooting reflex** – babies can distinguish the smell of their mother's breasts from those of other women and, if the baby's cheek or mouth is gently touched, they will turn in search of the nipple, this is known as 'rooting'.
- **The grasp reflex** – new-born babies can grasp objects very tightly and if the baby's palm is touched with an object they will grasp it automatically.
- **The sucking reflex** – some babies, even when still in the womb will suck their fingers and thumbs. Once born, they have an automatic reflex to suck and swallow when anything is put in their mouth.

Physical development

A new-born baby will change dramatically in terms of physical development before they reach 11 months of age. They will go from lying on their back to perhaps being able to crawl and possibly even walk before the end of their first year of life.

Birth to 3 months	3 to 6 months	6 to 9 months	9 to 11 months
Displays primitive reflexes. Lies on back. Head falls forward. Back arches. Recognizes bright lights and shiny objects. Is startled by loud, sudden noises. Recognizes the voice of their primary carer. By the time the baby reaches 3 months they will be able to lift their head and kick vigorously. They will be able to watch things intently and play with fingers and rattles.	The baby should now be able to control their head much better and will show an interest in grasping objects. They will be able to switch objects from one hand to the other and are likely to put objects into their mouth in order to explore.	Many changes will have taken place physically by the time the child reaches 6 months. It is likely that they will be able to roll from front to back and they may even be attempting to crawl.	This is the age whereby most children are usually mobile. Being mobile may be in terms of shuffling along on their bottom, crawling or walking. Children of this age should be able to sit unaided and will be interested in trying to reach, grasp and throw objects. Their arm and leg movements will gradually become more controlled.

Intellectual development

It is important that parents and carers understand the intellectual development of a child in order to be able to provide them with the stimulation necessary to keep their interest and build upon what they know.

Birth to 3 months	3 to 6 months	6 to 9 months	9 to 11 months
Displays the primitive 'rooting' reflex. They will recognize and search for familiar sounds and voices. Babies of this age can focus on objects up to a metre away. They enjoy imitating facial expressions and are adept at making eye contact at this age. They feel pain.	Babies of this age need to be stimulated. They enjoy bright lights and colours and are interested in their surroundings. Their coordination is improving and they are now adept at reaching for objects.	It is necessary to stimulate a child of this age with more complex and interesting toys and games to keep them amused. They are fascinated with the world around them and are keen to explore.	A child of this age will enjoy imitating others and will be able to clap their hands and wave goodbye. They will start to remember things and will have begun to build on their memory skills. They are beginning to learn a great deal through observation.

Language development

Babies will spend the first 11 months of their lives trying to make sense of language. They will begin by cooing and gurgling and gradually build on their language skills so that by the end of their first year they will be able to understand simple instructions and may be able to imitate certain sounds.

Birth to 3 months	3 to 6 months	6 to 9 months	9 to 11 months
At birth babies' language skills are limited to either crying, gurgling or cooing. They are easily settled with a reassuring, familiar voice.	Between the ages of 3 and 6 months babies chuckle and laugh when something pleases them. They are adept at recognizing sounds and they try to imitate the sounds they hear.	Babies of this age have now begun to 'babble' constantly. They are confident using sounds such as 'ah' and 'ee'.	By the time the child reaches their first-year milestone they will be able to understand simple instructions and be able to carry out these instructions such as 'wave bye bye'. They will have learnt how to imitate certain sounds such as those made by animals that is 'baa' and 'meow'. Their babble will now be constant.

Emotional development

Babies will use their entire body movements to express their pleasure particularly at enjoyable times such as when being fed or cuddled. By the time a child has reached 6 months of age they will begin to become more aware of the feelings of the people around them and will often appear distressed if someone around them is crying or laugh when they hear others laughing regardless of their inability to understand what is going on. It is important to remember that this behaviour is due to the fact that the child is *recognizing* rather than *feeling* the actual emotions.

Birth to 3 months	3 to 6 months	6 to 9 months	9 to 12 months
Babies first begin to start smiling at around the age of 5–6 weeks.	It usually takes a baby 5–6 months for them to realize that they only have one mother. Between these ages babies are extremely trusting and they enjoy being in contact with others.	Children of this age have begun to develop feelings of insecurity and may become distressed if their mother leaves their sight. They are now becoming more aware of people they do not know.	Emotionally a child of this age develops rapidly. They begin to enjoy being with familiar people more and more and are starting to show preferences. They enjoy playing simple games.

Social development

From the age of birth through to 12 months a baby will develop from initially recognizing their primary carer to recognizing other people and will be conscious of people they do not know. By the time a baby reaches 11–12 months they are usually still quite shy with strangers. Babies under the age of 12 months experience fluctuating moods and rely heavily on adults for reassurance.

Babies grow and develop very quickly and this is never more true than in the first year of their lives. During this time they will go from being defenceless individuals completely reliant on their carers to provide them with their essential requirements such as food, warmth and

Birth to 3 months	3 to 6 months	6 to 9 months	9 to 11 months
Babies of this age enjoy the close physical contact of their main carer and enjoy intimate routines such as feeding, cuddling and bathing.	Babies aged from 3 to 6 months are very aware of what is going on around them and are interested in socializing with others.	At this stage of their development babies enjoy imitating others and will often laugh when they hear others laughing even though they are unaware of why they are doing so. Their social skills may have developed to feeding themselves with finger foods and drinking from a cup with a spout.	Children heading towards their first-year milestone are often good at playing alone and will enjoy doing this for lengthy periods of time. They will have discovered music and will enjoy repetitive stories and nursery rhymes. They are now beginning to learn that experiences can be shared and that they have influence on and are influenced by others.

love to being able to recognize people and objects, sit up, stand up, crawl or may be walk, clap hands, wave good bye, show emotion and develop preferences.

The remaining sections of this chapter will cover the physical, intellectual, language, emotional and social development of children from 11 months old through to 16 years, however it is important to remember that there is a considerable 'overlap' in development of young children which is why each section up until the child reaches 5 years will have some repetition in the way the child develops. For example although some children may be able to walk before they reach their first birthday the developmental norms would show that most children will not master this task until between the ages of 13 and 18 months.

Exercise

Spend some time considering the physical, intellectual, language, emotional and social development of any babies you care for who are aged between birth and 11 months. Look at where their development is currently at and compare this to how they were when you first began caring for them. How do you anticipate their development to have changed in the next month or two?

8 to 20 months

Physical development

During the ages of 8 and 20 months a baby will usually have changed quite dramatically in terms of physical development. They will have mastered sitting, standing, crawling and walking and should be able to kneel without support and get to their feet using furniture to help them. They should be able to climb stairs under supervision with 2 feet at a time although they will find it difficult to maintain balance. They are usually adept at feeding themselves with finger foods and, towards the end of this period, they should be able to use a spoon successfully.

Intellectual development

Between the ages of 8 and 20 months a child's memory begins to develop rapidly and they will be able to recall past events. They are becoming more and more aware of their environment and are keen to learn and explore. It is necessary for parents and carers to provide interesting and stimulating activities to keep the child amused and to capture their imagination. Children of this age cannot see things from different points of view and can only focus on one aspect of a situation at a time, however they do understand that people think in different ways and that they have likes and dislikes.

Language development

Children under the age of 2 years have a limited vocabulary although they can often understand many more words that they can speak. Their language will progress from simple sounds and imitations such as 'moo' to basic words such as 'cat'. Children between the ages of 8 and 20 months usually babble constantly and often use expression. They enjoy making 'personal' words as they begin to develop their language skills.

Emotional development

A child aged between 8 and 20 months will usually enjoy socializing and they are happiest with people they know. They have learnt how to show preferences and interests and are becoming increasingly aware of the feelings of others. They often imitate the moods of others and their own feelings will fluctuate greatly. They are beginning to believe in themselves and are now developing self-confidence.

Social development

Children of this age are usually very sociable. They enjoy being around others although they can and should enjoy playing alone for periods of time. Towards the end of this stage they will be increasingly mobile and their curiosity will increase with the added advantage of being able to get around. From the age of approximately 12 months the child will have developed a sense of identity which will progress throughout the following months.

Exercise

Think about the physical, intellectual, language, emotional and social development of any children you are caring for who are aged between 8 and 20 months. How does their development compare to the way they were 2 months ago? In which areas have they made the most progress? Have they progressed at the rate you expected them to?

16 to 26 months

Physical development

The child will have now progressed from crawling to becoming confident on their feet. They will be able to run and climb and should be able to negotiate stairs with ease although this may still be with 2 feet at a time rather than by using alternate feet. They should be confident in kicking and throwing a ball although they may still find it difficult to catch one. They are gradually beginning to gain control of their whole bodies and are becoming aware of how to negotiate space and objects around them.

Intellectual development

The child will now have discovered many things for themselves and will be increasingly inquisitive about the world around them. They will have discovered 'pretend play' and will enjoy talking to themselves while playing in this way. They will have discovered music and will enjoy making sounds.

Language development

A child's speech develops rapidly by the time they reach the age of 2 years and it is thought that their vocabulary is now extended to around 50 words. They can however understand many more words and should be able to follow simple instructions. They should be confident taking part in conversations by the time they reach 26 months and will enjoy sharing songs and nursery rhymes.

Emotional development

A child's sense of identity will have progressed rapidly. They will be acutely aware of their feelings and should be able to describe how they are feeling. Emotions are very strong at this age and the child may have difficulty controlling them. They are beginning to take pleasure in learning new skills.

Social development

Social skills develop rapidly as the child enjoys being able to do more and more things for themselves. They should be confident dressing themselves and be able to carry out simple tasks. They should be able to feed themselves using a fork and spoon. They are now beginning to seek out others to share experiences.

Exercise

Look carefully at the children you care for who are aged between 16 and 26 months. How have these children progressed in terms of physical, intellectual, language, emotional and social development in the past 2 months? Has their rate of progression speeded up, slowed down or remained the same?

---

22 to 36 months

Physical development

By now a child should be able to negotiate stairs 1 foot at a time. They should be able to balance on 1 foot and be confident walking backwards and sideways. They should be able to walk and stand on tiptoes maintaining balance and jump from low heights. They should be confident climbing and may be able to ride a tricycle.

Intellectual development

Pretend play will continue and develop in children of this age. The child should now be able to sit for some time and take part in simple activities involving painting and crayoning. They should be able to control a pencil and may even be able to use a pair of scissors to cut paper.

Language development

Children of this age group should be able to communicate well. They will talk constantly and ask lots of questions. They will enjoy repetitive stories and may request them over and over again. They should be able to talk in sentences and use tenses and plurals. Children of this age can often become frustrated as their thinking can often overtake their ability to express themselves verbally.

Emotional development

Children should now be able to express themselves confidently. They are aware of gender differences. They should be able to dress themselves satisfactorily and go to the toilet independently. They are becoming more and more aware of the unknown and can be prone to becoming easily afraid of things they are unsure of as their imagination and emotions progress.

Social development

Children between the ages of 22 and 36 months should enjoy each other's company and towards the end of this age group they should be capable of making friends and playing alongside one another amicably. They are beginning to understand the importance of negotiation and taking turns although they will often resort to tantrums if they do not get their own way. They should now be capable of responding to the feelings and wishes of others.

Exercise

Consider the physical, intellectual, language, emotional and social development of the children in your care who are aged between 22 and 36 months. Have they progressed in some areas faster than in others? If so, which areas do you consider they have made the most progress in?

30 to 50 months

Physical development

By the time the child reaches 50 months their physical development will have increased rapidly. They are now capable of moving freely with confidence. They will be able to run, climb, jump and hop. They should be able to run up and down stairs using 1 foot at a time. They will be confident balancing on 1 foot and be able to walk along a straight line. They will be able to catch, kick, throw and bounce a ball and will be confident taking part in simple ball games. They should be able to negotiate space successfully.

Intellectual development

Children should now be able to draw recognizable objects. For example people and animals will consist of a body, head, legs etc. They should be able to carry out tasks involving fine motor skills such as confidently threading small beads onto a string. Their memory will be developing fast enabling them to be able to recall past events and to look forward to future ones.

Language development

Children of this age are very inquisitive and use their grasp of language to feed their inquisitiveness asking relentless questions. Words such as why, how, when and where are frequently used. They should be able to use simple statements and questions linked to gestures and be confident using intonation and rhythm. They should be capable of listening to stories with increasing attention and recall.

Emotional development

By the time a child reaches 50 months they will have begun to understand the complexities of emotion, however they will still find it difficult to control their emotions. Their imagination will be prolific and they may still be afraid of the unknown. They should now be taking a positive approach to events and activities and be confident linking up with others for guidance and support.

Social development

Children aged between 30 and 50 months will be aware of their own social backgrounds. They will understand the differences between gender and culture and will be keen to feel accepted. They enjoy being with other children and making friends. They understand the need for sharing and taking turns and are beginning to recognize right from wrong. Children of this age should be able to demonstrate flexibility and be able to adapt their behaviour to different social situations and routines.

Exercise

Consider the children in your care who are aged between 30 to 50 months. At what stage is their physical, intellectual, language, emotional and social development at? Are these stages in keeping with what you would expect to see at this age?

40 to 60 months

Physical development

Children of this age should be able to confidently use a wide variety of equipment such as skittles, skipping ropes and hoops. They should be able to play simple ball games and to skip and hop. Their balance should be good and they will enjoy moving to music. They should be capable of moving backwards and sideways. Their movements should be confident and show imagination. They should be capable of respecting the space of others and understand how to move around safely.

Intellectual development

Children should now be able to differentiate between real and pretend although they will still very much enjoy role play. They are increasingly becoming interested in the world around them and are keen to learn. They will begin to learn the concepts of numeracy and literacy and should be able to count with confidence and write letters and numbers. Their fine motor skills will continue to develop and their drawings will resemble the objects intended.

Language development

Children around the age of 60 months are usually confident speakers and they are adept at understanding the meaning of numerous words. They should know how to use language to gain attention, be capable of initiating conversations and know how to develop simple stories.

Emotional development

At this age a child should be confident in trying out new activities and initiating ideas. They should be able to maintain attention and concentration and be capable of valuing and contributing to their own well-being. They should be able to form good relationships with others.

Social development

Children aged between 30 and 50 months will be aware of their own social backgrounds. They will understand the differences between gender and culture and will be keen to feel accepted. They enjoy being with other children and making friends. They understand the need for sharing and taking turns and are beginning to recognize right from wrong. They should be capable of working as part of a group – to share fairly and work in harmony with others.

> **Exercise**
>
> Think about the children you are caring for who are aged between 40 and 60 months. How do you consider their physical, intellectual, language, emotional and social development has evolved over the past 6 months? Does their rate of development appear to have accelerated or do you think their development in some areas is slowing down? How far have the children progressed since you first started caring for them?

5 to 6 years

Between the ages of 5 and 6 years of age children are becoming increasingly aware of the world around them and are adept at independently completing every-day tasks such as dressing themselves, washing and eating.

Physical development

Children between the ages of 5 and 6 are confident hopping, skipping and dancing and they can take part in group ball games such as football and cricket. They have increased agility and are able to run, dodge and climb. Their balance and coordination will have improved greatly and they may now be able to ride a bicycle without the need for stabilizers. They will be able to touch their toes without bending their knees and will enjoy using a variety of play equipment such as swings, slides and climbing frames.

Intellectual development

Children of this age should be able to produce drawings with good detail for example a face with eyes, nose, mouth and hair. They should be able to recite their name, address and age. They are becoming more confident with literacy and numeracy skills and should be taking an active interest in reading and writing. They will begin to develop concepts of time and understand past, present and future. Towards the end of the sixth year children should be familiar with concepts of quantity and understand length, weight, measurement, distance, volume and capacity. They should be competent at jigsaw puzzles and be able to copy simple shapes.

Language development

Children of this age should be able to talk about past, present and future. Their speech should be fluent and grammatically correct with them being able to pronounce the majority of sounds. They will enjoy having stories read to them and become interested in reading simple text themselves. They should be able to recite nursery rhymes and songs.

Emotional development

Children between the ages of 5 and 6 years will have very definite likes and dislikes. They will be able to choose their own friends and will become more in control of their feelings. They will begin to understand how others may be affected by their behaviour and will instinctively help other children who may appear sad or distressed. Although they will now be able to distinguish between reality and fantasy they will often still become frightened by the unknown.

Social development

Children should now be able to carry out simple tasks such as tidying toys away and folding clothes. They should be completely independent at tasks such as washing and dressing themselves although they may still find it difficult to fasten shoelaces. They will be adept at choosing their own friends and will enjoy taking care of pets. They will have learnt that their own actions can have consequences on others and will show sympathy and forgiveness. They are beginning to grasp the concept of fairness and should be able to share and take turns.

6 to 8 years

From the age of 6 years children are beginning to have a clear sense of what is right and wrong and understand the importance of friendships. They are interested in numeracy and literacy and enjoy taking part in structured games with rules.

Physical development

By the time a child reaches the age of 6 to 8 years they will have mastered how to ride a two-wheeled bicycle confidently without the need for stabilizers. They will have increased stamina and will enjoy physical activities such as swimming and gymnastics. They will become skilful at catching and throwing a ball using both hands and one hand, and will be able to control their speed while running enabling them to swerve to avoid collision.

Intellectual development

They will be able to draw accurate detailed pictures and begin to introduce colour naturally. They should be competent with writing skills and be able to use both capital and small letters which are proportionate. Children between the ages of 6 and 8 years will enjoy the challenge of experimenting with new ideas and materials and will have mastered numeracy skills such as addition and subtraction. They should be able to perform simple calculations in their head and have a grasp of how to tell the time. The child should be able to use a computer mouse and keyboard to perform simple tasks.

Language development

Children should now know how to adequately express themselves using appropriate language. Their language will become more complex with a widening vocabulary. The child should be able to accurately describe objects and give opposite meanings.

Emotional development

Children of this age should be able to form close friendships. They enjoy engaging in cooperative play and should know how to control their emotions. They have begun to realize that they can keep their own thoughts private and are able to hide their true feelings. Many children of this age experience mood changes and quarrels often emerge due to the child becoming increasingly stubborn or demanding. Much importance is put on peer approval and the emphasis to succeed is apparent as the child begins to realize not only who they are but who they would like to be. They may become self-critical and express feelings of wonderment and admiration of others.

Social development

This is the time when children may become less sociable preferring to spend increasing amounts of time alone or with a special, valued friend. They have a clear sense of what is right and wrong but may resort to being argumentative or bossy.

Exercise

Are the children in your care who are aged between 5 and 8 years of age progressing in a way which would be considered 'normal'? Do some of the children show signs of needing additional help in some of the areas of development? If so, what do you consider you can do to help them?

8 to 12 years

Puberty can have a dramatic effect on the development of children. Girls usually experience the start of puberty between the ages of 9 and 13 years, however boys usually experience the start of puberty between the ages of 10 and 16 years. Peer pressure is immensely important at this age and much emphasis is put on being accepted which is why children of this age need to have the right clothes and create the right look. The onset of puberty has a marked effect on how the child feels about themselves and how they get along with others.

Physical development

Children aged between 8 and 12 years are beginning to show signs of an increase in body strength. They will be able to react to certain situations positively and will enjoy participating in energetic games and sports. They will become increasingly competitive and may find it difficult accepting defeat. Girls usually experience puberty before boys.

Intellectual development

Children will now be able to draw realistically introducing depth and shading. They will begin to join letters together to form handwriting and be able to write and draw with skill and dexterity. Their attention span should be increased and they should be confident expressing ideas. They should be able to plan ahead, explain what they are doing and use methods of evaluation. They should be confident readers and be able to use reference books as well as read text fluently. They should have the ability to think and reason and will enjoy taking part in numerous types of activities.

Language development

Children of this age group should be able to use and understand complex sentences. They will be quite verbal and should be confident in making up jokes or stories.

Emotional development

Children between the ages of 8 and 12 years are easily embarrassed. They take pride in their work and have an intense desire to be accepted. Peer pressure is very important. They have a growing sensitivity and are beginning to appreciate that others have feelings similar to their own although they will still have trouble understanding the needs of others. Their emotions are strong and intense and can often be conflicting as they emerge as argumentative 1 minute and responsive the next. They are beginning to understand the concept of loyalty and are capable of forming friendships easily although these friendships are sometimes changed rapidly as the child begins to look towards friendships based around similar likes to their own.

Social development

Children are now beginning to become acutely aware of the opposite sex although most friendships are still primarily based around the same gender. They appear to succumb to peer pressure readily as they are finding their feet and want to dress and act like their friends. They are particularly sensitive to criticism and become self-absorbed.

12 to 16 years

Between the ages of 12 and 16 years children are usually going through their period of adolescence. During this time both boys and girls will go through intense physical, psychological and emotional changes and it is very difficult to pin point what is actually 'normal' development and behaviour during this time, quite simply because adolescence affects all children differently.

Physical development

Physical development during this period of a child's life is known as 'puberty'. Puberty is the stage of growth whereby a child's body turns into that of an adult. Puberty starts with the release of hormones which are responsible for many changes in a child's body. Growth accelerates rapidly during this time hence the term 'growth spurt'. The head, feet and hands grow first followed by the arms and legs which not only grow in length but also in strength and finally the trunk of the body grows to full adult size and shape. Girls begin to develop breasts, grow taller and develop wider hips. They will start to menstruate most commonly between the ages of 12 and 13 years of age. Boys will begin to grow taller and become more muscular. Their voice will 'break' as a result of the body producing testosterone. They may begin to grow chest hair and, once the testicles begin to grow, they will also begin to produce sperm.

Intellectual development

Between the ages of 12 and 16 years of age there will be a noticeable difference in the thinking patterns of most children as they begin to think about possibilities. They will have the ability to think ahead, make plans and consider possibilities which are contrary to fact. They will start to question things which they may have previously taken for granted such as religion, politics or morality. They will be able to use imagination successfully when solving problems and will now be able to write swiftly and legibly. They should be reading and enjoying a variety of books and be able to approach a problem systematically.

Language development

Between the ages of 12 and 16 years a child's vocabulary should be immense. They will enjoy experimenting with the use of different and unfamiliar words although at times they may be used completely out of context. They should be able to express their own views and opinions and be confident debating issues which are of interest to them.

Emotional development

During this stage of development many children and teenagers are self-conscious. They may veer from acting childlike to behaving like an adult and they may be confused about their emotions. They often feel misunderstood as they struggle to come to terms with their own identity and strive to be liked and accepted. During the teenage years they tend to begin to separate from their parents more and more preferring to identify with friends as they become less dependant on family for affection and emotional support.

Social development

During the ages of 12 and 16 years children are able to think beyond themselves and are more able to take the feelings of others into account. They constantly seek approval and peer pressure is important to them. They are now becoming more socially skilled and are better able to resolve conflicts and work through situations amicably. As they are beginning to find themselves they will develop ideas and values of their own and may at times show challenging or unresponsive behaviour.

Exercise

Are the children in your care who are aged between 8 and 16 years developing into 'rounded' human beings who are showing signs of progress in physical, intellectual, language, emotional and social development and who are learning to take the feelings and wishes of others into consideration? Are they capable of making and maintaining lasting, meaningful friendships? Are there any areas in their development which are causing you concern?

2 Factors which Influence Child Development

This chapter directly relates to

- Unit 2 of the Diploma in Home-based Childcare: Childcare and Child Development (0–16) in the Home-based Setting
- Unit 5 of the Diploma in Home-based Childcare: Planning to Meet Children's Individual Learning Needs in the Home-based Setting
- The Learning and Development Requirements of The Early Years Foundation Stage

There are certain factors which will influence a child's development and these factors need to be recognized and understood by childcare practitioners in order for them to successfully monitor a child's development.

Some factors may be short-term such as a temporary loss of hearing, smell and taste due to a bad cold while others may have a long-term or even permanent effect on the child's development such as an accident leading to the loss of a limb or an illness such as cystic fibrosis.

The main factors which influence a child's development are:

- *Antenatal*: the condition of the child's mother prior to the birth of her child
- *Perinatal*: the actual birth of the child and includes premature and difficult births
- *Postnatal*: this involves factors after the child has been born such as diet, food allergies, accidents, health issues, etc.

Finally *behaviour* can have a monumental effect on a child's development and ability to learn. This chapter looks closely at these four factors which can influence a child's development.

Antenatal

The condition of the mother before the birth of her child has a big impact on the development of the child. Factors such as whether the mother smokes or consumes alcohol during her pregnancy have been shown, by scientific research, to affect her unborn baby. For example research suggests that mothers who smoke and drink during pregnancy generally give birth to smaller babies.

Antenatal care is essential for the health and well-being of the mother and to monitor the development of the baby. Mothers who receive good antenatal care are giving their unborn child the best start in life and reducing any potential risks they may encounter during their pregnancy. Antenatal care offers the mother:

- Routine checks
- Blood pressure monitoring
- Weight checks
- Urine checks
- Scans
- Monitoring of the baby's heartbeat
- The chance to ask questions and receive advice

Antenatal care offers the mother-to-be essential advice on maintaining a healthy lifestyle and preparing herself for the birth of her baby which will, hopefully, reduce the likelihood of them becoming anxious, worried or ill informed. Government guidelines change and often mothers who are having their second or subsequent babies, and who may feel they already know how to look after themselves and what to expect, may well find that advice has changed and antenatal care offers them up-to-date factual advice to help them through their pregnancy.

Perinatal

Perinatal involves the actual time of the birth, and factors which may influence a child's development during the perinatal period include premature births and difficult births. Premature babies are born early and are therefore not fully developed. The usual period of gestation for a full-term baby is between 38 and 40 weeks, a premature baby may be born between 24 and 37 weeks. Obviously the earlier a baby is born the less developed they will be, and this may result in low birth weights and developmental delays. Babies with low birth weights may be malnourished and their energy in the early months will be directed towards their physical rather than intellectual development. Premature babies are more susceptible to feeding difficulties and they may develop breathing problems. One of the most common problems suffered by babies born prematurely is their susceptibility to infection.

The problems which may be encountered during a difficult birth can also affect the development of a child though with medical advancement these risks have been significantly reduced over the years. Indeed the antenatal care a mother-to-be will receive should substantially reduce birth difficulties or, at the very least, it should enable doctors and midwives to anticipate any problems prior to the birth and allow them to put contingency plans in place so that they are prepared for any likely problems. Anoxia and hypoxia are however two of the most common birth difficulties which come about when the baby is deprived of oxygen during the birthing process. Anoxia means a total lack of oxygen to the baby at birth and hypoxia means that the child has been partially starved of oxygen. Oxygen deprivation is very serious and can cause a wide range of problems, all of which will affect the child's development such as cerebral palsy and learning difficulties.

Postnatal

Postnatal factors which may influence a child's development are numerous and may include:

- Accidents
- Breakdown of relationships/marriages
- Culture
- Diet
- Environment
- Health problems
- Lack of suitable stimulation
- Learning difficulties
- Loss or bereavement
- Sensory impairment

Accidents

Accidents can affect a child's development and, depending on the severity of the accident, this may be either permanent or temporary. An accident resulting in the loss of a limb, for example, may affect the way in which the child develops and the pace they develop at. For example the loss of a leg would impair the child's ability to stand, walk, run etc. whereas the loss of an arm will restrict the child's progress in writing, dressing, feeding themselves etc. Accidents may affect a child's social skills as they may be restricted in how they get out and about and mix with others which in turn may lead to withdrawal, uncertainty and a lack of confidence. Although injuries sustained during an accident may have a huge impact on the child's development and, in some cases, this impact may be permanent, it is possible to reduce the impact through thoughtful and sensitive care.

Breakdown of relationships/marriages

The breakdown of a relationship or ending of a marriage can have a serious impact on the social and emotional development of a child. Although much has been written about the breakdown of family life, and there have been arguments voiced regarding unhappy parents staying together for the sake of the child or splitting up due to a relationship becoming unbearable, the simple truth of the matter is that all children will be affected differently by the break up of their parents' relationship and it will probably be some time in the future before the real outcome can be acknowledged. Children feel secure, loved and safe in a happy, loving environment whether this is with one parent or two. If they are used to having both parents around and this setup comes to an abrupt end it is likely that the child will be affected. Although some children cope admirably in the face of adversity others will withdraw, become tearful and mistrusting. Although it should not always be assumed that the breakdown of a relationship will have an adverse effect on a child's development it is worth bearing in mind that young children often lack the comprehension to understand conflict between adults and they should never be drawn into arguments.

Culture

A child's culture can have a huge impact on their development. Cultural background must always be respected and childminders must support the children in their care to learn about and understand the cultures of others. Ignorance and scepticism will have a negative impact on the child's development and it is important for childminders to encourage children to learn about other cultures, languages, religions, family setups etc. in a positive way. Children need to feel valued and respected in order to build on their confidence and self-esteem and childminders can ensure this by showing a genuine interest in the child and providing a positive role model.

Diet

A healthy diet will provide a child with the nutrients and energy they need to grow and develop. Undernourished children or those who are not given a well-balanced diet may show signs of developmental delays. It is essential, as a parent or child care practitioner, that you provide children with a variety of healthy foods. In order for the body to grow and develop sufficiently it requires the following five nutrients:

- Fats
- Proteins
- Vitamins
- Carbohydrates
- Minerals

Fats help to provide the body with energy. A moderate amount of fat is necessary to maintain a healthy diet. Fats can be found in dairy products such as milk and cheese, meat, fish and vegetable oils.

Proteins are necessary to help the body to grow. Proteins also assist with the body's healing process and these can be found in meat, fish, soya, vegetables and, once again, dairy products such as milk and cheese.

Vitamins are essential for all types of growth and development and they can be found in many forms. Vitamins are derived from fresh food products such as fruit and vegetables.

Carbohydrates provide the body with energy. Carbohydrates can be found in bread, potatoes and vegetables.

Mineral elements are essential for the growth and development of the body. A lack of the iron element for example could lead to anaemia, and calcium is essential for strong bones and healthy teeth. The body's essential mineral elements can be found in dairy products such as milk and cheese (calcium), red meat and some green vegetables (iron).

There are five main food groups and these are:

- Dairy foods including milk
- Bread, cereals and potatoes
- Fruit and vegetables, of which it is recommended that we eat five portions a day
- Meat, fish, organic alternatives including pulses
- Fats and sugar

Many people have their own opinions with regard to food and while you may prefer, for example, to restrict or cut out completely your intake of red meat or food stuffs affected by chemicals or those which have been genetically modified it is important to remember that most families will have an opinion of the kind of diet they require their child to be fed and, wherever possible, childminders must take into consideration the wishes of the parents when it comes to planning suitable meals. Culture and religion may also play an important part in some diets as will the parent's attitudes towards sugar and fatty foods.

Environment

A child's environment plays an important part in all aspects of their growth and development. Poverty can have a detrimental effect. Poor housing and lack of money can affect a child's health and the amount of nutritional food they receive. A loving, secure environment where a child is made to feel loved and valued will have a much more positive effect on their growth and development than one where the child is unloved, unwanted and largely ignored.

Health problems

Most health issues can have an impact on the growth and development of children. Health problems can vary from relatively short-lived, common illnesses such as ear infections and colds to severe, life-threatening infections such as meningitis or cystic fibrosis. Other health issues which may affect a child's growth and development may stem from the child's diet and it is important to take into account the general well-being of the child and their energy levels. Tired, lethargic children will find it difficult to concentrate and therefore their development will be hindered.

Lack of suitable stimulation

All children need to be active, involved and inspired in order to grow and develop. Children should be provided with toys and activities suitable to their age and stage of development in order for them to learn and progress. Enthusiastic carers who offer inspirational stimulation are more likely to inspire children to learn and develop.

Learning difficulties

Learning difficulties such as hyperactivity, autism or speech and language problems will affect the way in which a child develops. The severity of the learning difficulty will of course determine how the child's ability to develop is affected. Any childminder who thinks that a child in their care may have a learning difficulty must discuss their concerns with the child's parents immediately and suggest that they seek expert help and advice.

Loss or bereavement

Although loss or bereavement can have a profound effect on children it is important to remember that children can have difficulty putting this concept into prospective. For example the loss of a favourite teddy bear or moving schools can be just as traumatic to a child as the death of a close family relative. Some children simply cannot understand the finality of bereavement and will often ask when they will see the bereaved person again. Although some children cope admirably when faced with this kind of trauma others may hide their feelings and resort to bottling things up. Consequently their development may suffer as they show their emotions in other ways such as becoming withdrawn, aggressive or disruptive.

Sensory impairment

Babies rely heavily on their senses to give them information about the world around them. They build on their information using sight, smell, touch, sound and taste, therefore a severe impairment of one or more of the senses could have a dramatic effect on the child's development. Regular health checks at birth should pick up on permanent, severe impairments however it is important to remember that temporary impairments to the senses may also have an effect on a child's short-term development such as a temporary loss of hearing following a cold or an ear infection.

Behaviour

The way in which a child behaves can have a huge influence on their development. Behaviour which goes unchecked in children who are not given appropriate boundaries can have a detrimental effect on their development.

All children need boundaries in order for them to feel valued and accepted. Boundaries put a limit on behaviour and enable a child to understand what is acceptable and what is not. At times a child's behaviour may fall short of our expectations and they may show signs of unacceptable behaviour.

It is important that all parents and childcare practitioners understand that there is a *reason* for all behaviour but, before we can successfully help a child to change their behaviour, we first need to understand it.

There are many reasons why a child may show unwanted behaviour and the list below outlines some of the reasons why a child may resort to misbehaving. The child may feel:

• Tired	• Misunderstood
• Anxious	• Restricted
• Bored	• Frightened
• Hungry	• Undervalued
• Frustrated	• Uncomfortable
• Unwell	• Unhappy

They may also be:

- Testing the boundaries
- Exploring their environment
- Unsure of what is expected of them
- Attention seeking
- Unaware that their behaviour is unacceptable
- Mimicking others

Children who are allowed to run amok and who have little regard for other people and their belongings will quickly become unpopular and unwelcome. It is essential that boundaries are set in order for all the children in the setting to feel valued and welcome and so that everyone can enjoy the opportunities for learning and development without individuals spoiling things for others.

Boisterous children, with high levels of energy, need to learn to control themselves and to learn when to let off steam and when to sit quietly and listen to what is being said. Children will not learn if they continually disregard what they are being told and have little or no consideration for others.

Children are not born with an understanding of how to behave. Babies and children need to learn how to behave and this is done through interaction. The learning process takes many years and is a continual progression. As a child gets older and more independent they should be allowed more freedom to experience, to make choices and learn through their mistakes.

Children learn how to behave in several ways:

- From their parents and carers as role models
- Through effective behaviour management
- From other people, friends, family, teachers etc.
- Television, films, newspapers etc.

It is absolutely essential that parents and practitioners decide on an effective method of managing a child's behaviour in order for the child to develop into a well-adjusted, acceptable member of the community. Behaviour has a huge effect on the way a child will form friendships and, later in life, relationships, their social success and their academic success. By the time a child starts school they should have a good grasp of acceptable behaviour and know what is and is not socially acceptable. Although it is highly likely that they will still misbehave from time to time they should need less guidance from the teacher in this respect and, in theory, will therefore be more ready to learn and more likely to succeed academically.

Exercise

Think about your own ideas of acceptable behaviour. How do you expect children to behave? Do you consider the behaviour of boys to be different to that of girls? How do you think your own behaviour was managed when you were a child? Do you consider your parents to have been too strict or too lenient? Have your own childhood experiences of behaviour management altered the way you expect children to behave?

3 Providing Play and Other Learning Experiences for Children in a Home-based Setting

This chapter directly relates to

- Unit 1 of the Diploma in Home-based Childcare: Introduction to Childcare Practice
- Unit 2 of the Diploma in Home-based Childcare: Childcare and Child Development (0–16) in the Home-based Setting
- The Welfare Requirements of The Early Years Foundation Stage

It is absolutely essential when working as a childminder, that you understand the importance of meeting children's individual needs in all areas of your work. A childminder's day can often be hectic with deadlines to meet for taking and collecting children from school, attending play group and nursery and taxiing children to and from various clubs. However, in addition to carrying out these routine obligations and meeting each child's basic physical and health needs, you will also be required to think about how you will:

- Create a welcoming environment
- Create enjoyable experiences for the children to play and learn from
- Ensure that all the children are respected
- Give the children the freedom of choice
- Ensure that all the children are treated with equal concern

Occasionally, you may not be able to meet the wishes of some of the children simply due to the fact that you are caring for others and, if this is the case you need to explain to the child, and if necessary, their parent, why this is the case. Children and adults need to work together and recognize that, while every effort will be made to respect the freedom and choice of each and every child, on some occasions they may need to learn to understand that it is not always possible to meet every request and sometimes their individual needs may need to take second place.

Planning for children's individual needs in the home-based setting

If you sit and think about the number of plans you make on a daily basis you would probably be amazed at your findings. Everyone makes plans every day. These plans are unlikely to be written down but our everyday lives are based on short- and long-term plans. Important events such as a wedding or birthday party are often planned well in advance with lists of things to do, guests to invite and outfits to wear. Everyday routines such as shopping trips and cooking meals are also planned. Before we can begin to bake a cake for example we need to check that we have the right ingredients and make a list of what we need to buy. Of course not all of the plans we make every day are methodical in this way. You may start your day mentally planning what you are about to do. Get up, have a shower, get dressed, eat breakfast, wash up, make the bed, etc. A large part of a childminder's day may be taken up with school, nursery and play group runs, nappy changing and feeding. However, the times in between need to be planned carefully in order to enable the childminder to put some structure into their day and for the children to benefit from suitable activities and experiences rather than to spend the day being ferried about, fed and changed with little or no quality time for playing and learning.

Childminders need to know how to plan their day so that the activities and experiences they offer the children enable them to experience variation in order for them to benefit from their time in the setting. Planning our day enables us to look carefully at the activities on offer and to ensure there is sufficient time to carry out the intended activities in order for the children to gain something from the experience. For example there is little point in deciding to have a baking session with the children at 3.00 p.m. if you have to leave to collect children from school at 3.20 p.m. The activity will either be rushed or abandoned both of which will be of no benefit to the children. In order for this activity to be a success and for the children to enjoy and learn from it the childminder needs to plan sufficient time to bake including considering how long it will take to weigh and mix the ingredients, how long the ingredients will take to cook and how long it will take to clear away and wash up.

Although planning is vital when considering children's individual needs it is also important to understand the whole of the planning *cycle* including being able to implement the plans and decide whether they are suitable for the children. Childminders need to:

Plan

Think carefully about the children in your care; their ages, their abilities and their preferences. What type of activities do you consider to be beneficial for them? There is little point in preparing to bake a cake if the children you are caring for are too young to help. Likewise providing baby toys and rattles for a three-year-old will not go down well.

Implement

Think carefully about the activities you have planned and decide on the best time for the children to take part in each. Make sure there is sufficient time for the children to actively take part without rushing them. Try to avoid planning complex activities at a time of the day when the children are likely to be too tired to enjoy them.

Observe and assess

It is crucial we observe and assess the children to ensure that the activities are suitable for the children they are aimed at. Is the activity too hard or too easy? Do the children appear to be enjoying what they are doing? Are they actively involved? Are they bored?

Evaluate

Finally, after observing and assessing the children while they are taking part in the activity you have planned, you should be able to decide whether the activity has been a success or not. Can the activity be expanded upon? Would you consider repeating the activity? If not, why not? Can the activity be improved?

It is important to remember that not all planning results in endless paperwork. Planning can be just as effective if it is done informally and, experienced childminders are usually planning instinctively with great success. One of the responsibilities of a childminder is to provide the children in their care with the best start to their early education and this can be done with careful thought about the activities they provide which will give them a head start in learning while having fun and will follow through to their formal school years. One of the main reasons parents choose a childminder to care for their child, over a nursery, is that they can offer everyday learning experiences which educate children while they are having fun. Simple tasks such as setting the table and sorting laundry can be useful to promote early numeracy; pairing socks, sorting colours, counting how many knives, forks and spoons are needed etc. Not only do these tasks encourage a child's early education they do so while helping them to develop in every way rather than in the formal setting of a nursery or classroom.

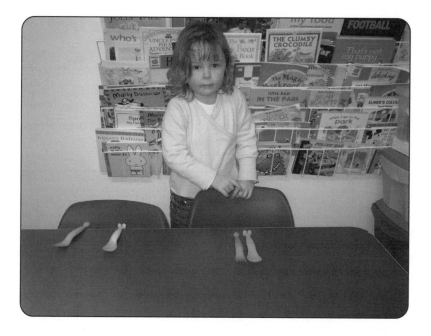

Talking to children, encouraging them to do things for themselves, listening to what they have to say and valuing their opinions are much more important to a child's learning than providing expensive educational toys and worksheets. There are many ways in which child-minders can 'educate' the children in their care and these methods can and should be done all day, every day and they include:

- **Good communication:** talking to the children while you are doing tasks together is one of the most important methods of teaching. Whether the child is trying to feed themselves, is learning to potty train or trying to master how to tie shoelaces it is vital that you talk to them as all children learn through communication.
- **Providing first-hand experiences:** children need to be involved and to experience things for themselves. Childminders need to provide a safe environment with appropriate activities and resources for first-hand experiences to be enjoyed.
- **Giving the children your time:** the most important thing you can provide for the children in your care is your undivided attention. True, children need to learn to play together and alone at times however, the support and guidance of an adult role model is invaluable. You must show genuine interest in what the child is saying and doing and take an active part in their games and learning opportunities.

Although I have mentioned earlier in this chapter that not all planning needs to be written down and often the paperwork in the childminding profession can be daunting, you may find it more effective to record some of your planning. By building up a collection of planned activities and recording them, you will be able to refer to them in the future. Written records of your planned approach to the children's learning are also useful to show your Ofsted inspector who may well ask for evidence on how you plan your play and other activities during your inspection.

Exercise

Think about an average day in your own life. What things do you plan for on a daily basis? How many of these things do you make written plans for and how many do you rely on your memory for?

Planning is very personal. No two childminders will plan their play and learning opportunities in the same way quite simply because we are all unique and we will be caring for children who are also unique. The abilities and needs of each child may differ enormously and effective planning will take into account each child's personal requirements. There is no right or wrong way to plan your day providing the method you choose is effective. Whether you prefer to use written plans or keep your ideas in your head it is important that you *share* the information with the parents and the children you care for. Ask for their ideas and opinions and involve them as much as possible.

It is important for practitioners to understand the difference in short, medium and long-term plans in order to understand how to plan their work. Initially you will need to work out, with the child's parents, exactly what you are hoping to achieve with the planned activity. For example you could be trying to teach a child how to recognize the four primary colours. Your final goal will be to get the child to recognize these colours however before reaching this 'long-term' goal you will have set yourself a 'short-term' and 'medium-term' goal which, once they have been achieved will enable the child to reach the 'long-term' goal of recognizing the primary colours. You will need to decide on a time frame for achieving each of the goals, the length of which will be dependent on the complexity of what you are hoping the child will learn. A short-term plan may cover a week, medium-term a month and finally, after 6 months you may have achieved your long-term goal.

Some childminders find it easier to plan their activities around a topic or theme. This can be a very effective method of planning providing the children you care for are old enough to understand the topic or theme and you have sufficient children in your setting to make the learning experiences enjoyable. It is important that childminders do not allow topics and themes to restrict how the children learn and that they still allow plenty of opportunity for spontaneous play.

Planning and providing care for mixed age groups

One of the most important, and often difficult, aspects of a childminder's job is being able to successfully plan and provide care and suitable activities and learning experiences for children of mixed age groups. Many childminders will care for children of school age in addition to babies and pre-school children. Although it is true to say that, on most days, the school age children will be spending the majority of their day away from the childminding setting while they are in school, it is important to think carefully about how you will provide adequate stimulation and resources for these children both before and after school and during school holidays. Older children should not be expected to take second place and to have their play restricted because of the younger ones although there may be times when older children will need to consider the ages of the younger ones when requesting certain activities.

Childminders need to carefully consider the toys, books and other resources they provide and make sure that these are suitable for *all* the ages and stages of development of the children they are caring for. For example eight-year-olds should not be expected to play with baby and toddler toys and teenagers should not have to make do with immature reading material.

All children learn through play and first-hand experiences and it is the duty of the childminder to provide each child with sufficient resources which are appropriate to their age and stage of development in order to provide entertaining and stimulating experiences. Although the way in which the childminder plans their day and the activities they provide influences the way in which the children play and learn other factors also have an effect such as the number and ages of the other children in the setting and the amount of quality time the childminder actually spends interacting with the children are very important factors.

All children need their play and learning activities to be planned and structured. This includes young babies and toddlers as well as older children. The activities, resources and experiences you provide must be appropriate to the age and stage of development of each individual child in your care and children should not be expected to 'make do' with what you have if these items are clearly unsuitable.

When considering what resources to provide for older children who may be in your setting before and after school and during the holidays it is important to remember that most children will have had their fill of the classroom by the time they are with you and therefore it is neither appropriate nor necessary for you to mirror the activities they are doing within the classroom environment. It is possible for you to 'support' the child's learning in a fun as well as educational way providing you understand the basics of the school curriculum. By familiarizing yourself with the curriculum and developing your own understanding you should be able to support the children with their homework. Caring for school age children should never be seen as the easy option. Although babies can be very demanding and their routines of feeding, changing and sleeping may be restricting older children can be equally demanding and they should never be expected to be left to their own devices while you concentrate on caring for the younger ones.

Many childminders find it very challenging balancing the care of mixed age groups of children and, providing activities and resources to keep everyone happy, although essential, can be difficult. You need to be realistic about the number of children you can cater for and always remember that the number of children you are registered to care for is your *maximum* amount and not your *target* amount. If you do not feel confident filling all your places then don't. Take on the children you know you can care for adequately and, if you feel the time is right at a later date, add to your numbers slowly. You may be caring for a very demanding child who needs more of your time than you expected and it would therefore be very unfair to stretch yourself too far by taking on other children simply because your registration allows you to do so.

Older children are just as needy of your time as the younger ones, albeit in different ways. Although they will not need feeding and changing they will need encouragement when tackling personal hygiene and self-help skills. Children who are about to start school can be prepared for the transition by encouraging them to gain independence in self-help skills for example going to the toilet independently, being able to fasten coats and shoes and wash their hands effectively. This will boost their self-confidence and prepare them for the challenges ahead.

Caring for school-age children

It is important to look carefully at the issues school-age children face such as bullying and stranger danger and try to develop their knowledge and understanding of how to cope with these situations through both planned and unplanned activities while the children are in your care. Consider role play to help to highlight these kinds of scenarios and always be prepared to give your time and attention to a child who may be experiencing any such problems.

Often school children will have homework. It can be quite difficult for childminders to insist that a child does their homework while they are in their setting and it should not be expected by the parents that this will happen. By all means if the child is happy to knuckle down and get the work done then you should be there for them to offer support and encouragement however, it is not the job of a childminder to force a reluctant child to do their homework. Always bear in mind that the child has just spent the whole day in a classroom and may well be ready for a rest and will be hoping to spend some time winding down and playing when they reach the childminder's setting. Speak to the child's parents and try to work out a suitable strategy which works well for everyone. Often parents will prefer their child to do their homework at home where the distractions are fewer and when they themselves can devote the time to help and encourage their own child. However, some children spend a lot of time in the childcare setting and may be too tired to do their homework once they have got home. If this is the case, but the child is reluctant to do their homework with you and you find yourself with a battle of wills on your hands, then you must speak to the child's parent in order to work out a strategy which will work well for everyone. The job of ensuring that homework is completed on time is the ultimate duty of the parent. Providing you make it clear that you are able and willing to help the child and that you ensure there is a quiet place for homework to be done away from the younger children you will be fulfilling your obligations.

When considering planning activities and providing resources for mixed age groups of children there are a certain number of important factors which you must take into account:

- **Always think carefully about the number and ages of the children you are caring for and ensure that you have sufficient resources for *all* of the children to play.** Young children should not be expected to play with toys which are unsuitable for their age and stage of development and, likewise older children should not be expected to play with toys inappropriate to their level of development.
- **Take into account each individual child's interests and try to cater for their preferences as well as their needs.** This is not to say that you should be expected to provide every 'fad' on the market. However if you have a little boy who is particularly interested in creative activities try to provide a range of different materials for him to experiment with. This need not be expensive and often simple junk modelling will suffice.
- **Talk to the child's parents and always take their wishes into account.**
- **Think about the needs of all of the children in your care.** Do you care for any children will disabilities? If so, you must make sure that they are able to take part in all the activities you provide and it is your duty to ensure that this is possible.
- **Consider how you will encourage diversity and equality.** It is not acceptable to choose an activity and force every child in your setting to take part. Children should be allowed freedom of choice but it is paramount that you treat each individual with equal concern and fairness and that you ensure that all children have their individual needs met.
- **Think carefully about health and safety when providing activities and resources for mixed age groups of children.** For example older children may happily engage in construction activities involving 'lego' bricks however these tiny bricks are totally unsuitable for toddlers and babies as they would pose a choking hazard should they put them in their mouths. It is your duty to ensure that all the children are safe while embarking on activities and that the resources you provide are suitable for their age and stage of development.

Homework aside, children who have spent all day at school, particularly those in reception class who are just getting used to a long, structured day, may well be exhausted when they reach your setting. Some children are hungry and ready to sit down, eat and relax while others may be excited and full of pent-up energy which they have had to suppress while in the classroom. It is important to take your cue from the children and to cater for their needs individually, wherever possible. Provide a quiet area for young ones to settle down with a book or watch a favourite television programme after a busy day. Plan suitable activities for those children who still have the energy to play and take the time to support children who have homework to complete. Before and after school times can be very hectic. You will have a lot of children on your premises most of which will need breakfast or tea and all with their own needs and preferences which you will be expected to meet. With time and experience this will become easier, however it is careful planning which will make this time happy and enjoyable for everyone.

School holidays should be fun times. Children need to leave their school work behind and take a well-earned break. It is your job, as a childminder, to make the holidays special for the children in your care and, as you will not have school times to adhere to, this is the ideal time to plan trips and outings and to indulge in those activities which may be more time consuming and messy.

Plan the school holidays carefully and you should be able to cater for the needs of all the children and keep them all happy and entertained. Make the most of your local amenities and consider taking the children to the local park or sports centre.

Exercise

Spend some time planning for the next school holiday. Make a list of the number of children you will be providing care for and their ages. Source local amenities to find out what is happening in your area and consider which events are suitable for the children you are caring for. Will you need to make any special arrangements to enable you to take part in your chosen activities if so, what considerations do you need to make?

Personal, Social and Emotional Development 4

Chapter Outline

This chapter directly relates to

- Unit 2 of the Diploma in Home-based Childcare: Childcare and Child Development (0–16) in the Home-based Setting
- The Learning and Development Requirements of The Early Years Foundation Stage

Affectionate 'bonds' are very important for promoting personal security, emotional well-being and warm relationships. For children to develop and grow satisfactorily they need to feel loved and valued. 'Bonding' usually begins immediately after the birth of a baby, providing the parents have immediate contact with the child. This bond is then developed throughout the early months of the baby's life and it is easy to see how children become attached to certain people by the way they communicate with them, often becoming clingy or excited after a short separation.

Children need to develop their personal, social and emotional needs in order to become valued members of society, make friends and eventually forge lasting, meaningful relationships. It is absolutely crucial that childcare practitioners are confident about ensuring that children have a secure environment which will promote their personal, social and emotional well-being. If childminders get it wrong they risk having unhappy, insecure children in their setting which will be of benefit to no-one. Children who are not happy and secure will not reach their full potential and other learning opportunities, however well planned and thought through will be of little use.

Personal development is about learning self-help skills such as using a toilet independently and being able to dress and undress. Social development includes learning how to interact with other people, how to make friends and build relationships. Emotional development is about learning how to recognize, express and deal with emotions and feelings.

Dispositions and attitudes

As with many areas of a child's development much will be learned from their parents and carers. It is important to remember that parents are the most important and influential people in a child's life and their initial attitudes and opinions will be formed as a direct result of those of their main carer. It is therefore very important that we do not impose our own opinions and preferences onto the children we are caring for even if this is unintentional. Expressing our own thoughts and opinions may have a negative effect on a child, particularly if your views and opinions differ from those expressed at home by their parents.

All children are different and as such they should be treated as individuals and with equal concern. No two children will have the same disposition or attitudes; some children may be quite obstinate and demanding for example while others appear laid back and easy going. It is important that childminders understand the necessity of allowing children the freedom to express themselves adequately and as individuals.

All children should be encouraged to have positive attitudes towards other people and situations. A defeatist nature can be very bad for a child's confidence and esteem and it is the job of the childminder to ensure that children are encouraged to rise to a challenge and to give their best.

Encouraging a child to have a positive disposition where they have a happy outlook and attitude will support them in their learning. Positive dispositions enable children to take an interest in what is happening around them, to become involved, to be curious, persist if they are uncertain and take responsibility all of which will help them to learn and develop.

Supporting a child's personal, social and emotional development should be automatic for a caring, nurturing childminder. It should not be seen as a learning objective but should, quite simply, be a way of life, an ethos. Every aspect of your work should be focused on how best you can boost a child's confidence and self-esteem and how you can help them to achieve success which will, in turn, enable them to feel proud of themselves.

Self-confidence and self-esteem

For children to succeed they need to be reassured. Children often lack confidence and their self-esteem can easily take a battering if they have tried, and failed, to carry out a task. Every child who starts in your setting will be at a different stage in their development. Likewise each will have varying levels of self-esteem and confidence. Some children may be used to change and tackle the challenges of a new setting in their stride, confident with new surroundings they may quickly make friends. However others may take weeks or even months to build up their confidence and mix freely with others. Children need to feel valued in order for their self-confidence and self-esteem to improve and often they will pick up negative feelings about themselves. All children need to feel they belong and are valued members of their community and often, in cases of racial or sexist remarks, it can take a long time to repair any damage done to the child's confidence. Parents and carers who are critical of their children and not forthcoming with praise and encouragement can have a negative impact on their children who will often fear failure and be unwilling to attempt something in case they do not live up to the expectations.

Having self-esteem enables a child to express themselves, alter situations, embrace their success and learn from their mistakes. Self-esteem is impossible to 'teach'. It needs to be shown right from the start of the child's life and continued throughout their childhood if they are to grow into confident adults eager to tackle challenges and embrace new opportunities.

Childminders have a duty to seek out the best in each individual child and to praise their efforts and show pride in their achievements no matter how small or inconsequential they may seem. A child who has mastered putting on his own coat for the first time for example, after perhaps days of struggling, will be proud of themselves. If the adults around him fail to notice and praise his achievements he will quickly begin to wonder why he bothered and may even be reluctant to try anything else. In the long-term, if praise is never forthcoming, he will begin to feel useless and his efforts unworthy of praise. His self-esteem will be deflated and his confidence will be greatly affected. By taking the time to acknowledge the child's achievements, a few simple words of encouragement, you will boost his confidence, give him pride in himself and encourage him to carry the task out every day encouraging his need for growing independence which will, in turn, lead him to try other things for himself. The outcome in this case will be very different.

In order for children to feel valued and respected they need to see positive images of children like themselves and families like their own on display. Childminders need to make sure that they provide positive images and resources which show children and families from all walks of life in positive roles. Images of men and women in non-traditional gender roles such as male nurses and female fire-fighters can be used to show diversity and encourage children to accept people as individuals. Disabled people should be shown in positive roles and each child's unique family and cultural background should be embraced and celebrated enabling the child to discover and enjoy being who they are.

The attitudes and values we show to the children in our care will have a profound effect on them and it is therefore crucial that childminders never criticize or speak derogatively about the child, their family or their background. Remember that facial gestures and body language can often say as much as the spoken word and we must keep these in check at all times.

Before a child starts school their self-esteem and confidence is formed exclusively by their family and carers. Other influences usually take effect once the child has started nursery or primary school when outside forces come into the equation. Confident children may take everything in their stride as their self-esteem will effectively protect them from the opinions of others, however those children with little or no confidence will experience nagging doubts and this will affect their ability to enjoy school and learn from the experiences available. In order for a child's confidence to grow and for them to feel valued they need to:

- Be able to express their feelings freely
- Have these feelings acknowledged positively

Ask anyone what they would most like in life and you will probably get a list of half a dozen things; health, money, good job, family etc., however it is probably true to say that somewhere on that list will be 'happiness'. Most parents would put 'happiness' on the top of their wish list for their children. This is because, generally speaking, happiness is what motivates individuals. Being happy boosts confidence and self-esteem; it ensures positive relationships, triggers motivation and produces well-balanced capable human beings.

Whoever we are and wherever we come from we all have a universal desire to feel valued and accepted and young children are no different from adults when it comes to wanting to be accepted, valued and loved. By nurturing this need at a young age we are effectively setting up the child for life, encouraging them to express themselves, communicate effectively and listen and respond to the needs of others.

Tips for boosting self-esteem in children

- Make sure that you value *all* the children in your setting and that you value them for *who* they are not what they can do or how they look.
- Ensure that the messages you give out are *positive* ones and that you never judge people because of their gender, disability, skin colour, race, religion etc.
- Praise children's achievements no matter how small these may be.
- Respect the children in your care and their families.
- Encourage the children to try new experiences.
- Never ridicule a child for trying and failing. Praise the *effort* more than the result.
- Allow children freedom of choice while taking into account safety.
- Provide the children with a positive role model at all times.
- Provide the children with clear, fair and consistent boundaries, so that they are aware of what is expected of them at all times.
- Show children that you value and trust them.

Forming relationships and interacting with others

Children go through different stages of play. These stages are:

- **Solitary play:** from the ages of birth to 2 years most children will play alone.

- **Spectator play:** from the ages of 2 to 3 years most children will enjoy watching other children play but will rarely join in.
- **Parallel play:** again from the ages of 2 to 3 years children will play alongside one another but rarely will they play together.
- **Associative play:** between the ages of 3 and 4 years children are beginning to form friendships. They may occasionally play cooperatively.
- **Cooperative play:** once a child reaches the age of 4 years they are usually able to play cooperatively and support one another.

Although it is important that children see you and the other adults in their lives as being caring and cooperative it is equally important that they extend these thoughts and feelings towards the other children in the setting. For adults to command respect from the children they must also show it and by showing respect to the children they will, in turn, learn to respect themselves and each other. This is a very important learning curve which some children will grasp quicker than others. Relating to others, interacting and forming friendships are very important parts of a child's social development. Children will need to learn to share, take turns, listen to and take into account the feelings and preferences of others if they are to be valued, respected and included.

One of the key factors for children learning to form relationships is communication and having the ability to recognize how they feel. Children need to feel accepted in order for them to forge meaningful friendships. Childminders need to think carefully about how they can encourage children to form effective relationships both with the other children in the setting and with adults. Children should be encouraged to take their time to get to know others, to communicate with them and show sensitivity.

Sharing and taking turns is an important part of building friendships and, although this will come easy to some children, others find it difficult and can often resort to being mean and throwing tantrums as they do not fully understand the consequences of their actions or the need for them to cooperate. It is pointless for the childminder to tell the child to 'wait their turn' or 'let David have a go now' if they are not prepared to explain *why* it is necessary for them to do so.

Exercise

Think about your own attitude to making friends and maintaining friendships. Do you consider friendships to be important? Consider the friends you have, how often do you see them? How long have you known them? What attributes do you think make a good friend? Why do you think some people have more friends than others? What do you think makes a person more popular?

Dealing with emotions and self-control

Behaviour has to be learnt. Children are not born with the ability to know right from wrong nor are they born good or bad. Positive role models and reasonable boundaries which have been well thought through are the best ways of helping to promote positive behaviour in the childminding setting. We have probably all witnessed a child at some point complain about another saying they refuse to play with them because they are 'mean' or because they always want to win or go first. The childminder who expects every child in their care to know right from wrong, to always share and take turns and who will happily relinquish first place for another child is in for a shock! Young children love to be the first, to win, to be better than their peers. It is human nature to want to be the best and to succeed and children are no exception. Most children are competitive and love to beat their friends. This is all part of growing up and healthy competition should be encouraged. However it is when this competition starts to get out of hand and a child cannot enjoy the game or task unless they come first that you will start to have problems. It is important to praise *all* the children not just the winner and to make sure that everyone enjoys taking part even those who are clearly not as adept and have little chance of achieving first place. Providing they are not ridiculed and their efforts are praised and valued they will benefit from taking part.

Often young children have difficulty in self-control. Emotions can be very powerful and thinking about their actions and the consequences of them are not usually a priority for young children. If they want something they do not usually see the need to wait and rarely put things in perspective. Frustration and anger lead to loss of self-control as does being upset or frightened. Children need to be listened to and their opinions and wishes taken into account in order for them to feel settled and calm. This in turn will reduce the number of occasions when they may lose control and lash out.

Some children may find it difficult to express their feelings appropriately and this may result in them appearing uncooperative, aggressive or withdrawn. Toddlers are particularly prone to this as they appear confident and want to do many things for themselves, however they often lack the language skills to express themselves adequately. Children of this age also lack any sense of danger and cannot understand the reasons for them taking care, waiting, holding hands etc.

It is important that children are allowed the freedom to express *all* emotions and as a childminder you may need to take a back seat at times and allow children to work things out for themselves. Obviously happy children who are laughing and enjoying themselves will not be any cause for concern; however you should resist the urge to intervene immediately if children get cross with each other. Obviously if the situation deteriorates into physical violence or if one of the children is clearly upset or unhappy then you may be required to diffuse the situation but, whenever possible, try to allow the children to work things out for themselves in order for them to experience all types of emotions. Physical violence and withdrawn silence are both difficult emotions for children and childminders to handle however by encouraging the children to talk about their feelings and allowing them to express themselves freely, in a safe atmosphere, you will hopefully help to eliminate these negative emotions.

Self-care

For children to become independent they need to learn how to master self-care tasks. Their confidence and self-esteem will take a leap when they master simple tasks for themselves. This is particularly helpful when children are beginning to start nursery or reception class. Children should be encouraged to take pride in their own appearance and this can be extended by allowing them reasonable choices when it comes to choosing clothes. For parents to allow their child to express their likes and dislikes they are acknowledging that they have opinions which are valued.

Self-care tasks include a number of areas of personal hygiene for a child to successfully manage. All the tasks will develop the child's independence and lead to added self-esteem. Being able to carry out personal hygiene tasks independently is a great boost to a child's confidence. Children need to learn how to manage:

- Going to the toilet independently
- Dressing and undressing themselves
- Washing hands satisfactorily
- Wiping their own nose
- Washing their own face
- Brushing teeth
- Brushing hair

Exercise

Although self-care skills are important many young children find some of these tasks difficult to m aster and can become frustrated while trying. Think about ways in which you can break down the aforementioned tasks into manageable steps and how you can make learning the tasks fun rather than tedious.

Sense of community

Feelings of belonging are paramount to a child's well-being and emotional development. We live in a multicultural society whose values are constantly changing. Children need to learn to be socially adept, to live in harmony and acceptance of others and to value others. No child should be made to feel less worthy than another and you should be encouraging children to accept and appreciate the differences in others rather than to judge or criticize. Ignorance breeds contempt and fears and misconceptions usually come about through a lack of knowledge and understanding.

It is vital that childminders encourage and embrace the understanding of other cultures and that they introduce these into their setting.

Balancing children's growing needs for independence with the need to keep children safe

There is a fine line between keeping children safe and suffocating them with over protection. Children need to be able to strive for independence while remaining safe and this is not always an easy task for parents and childminders.

A young child's need for independence takes into account their eagerness to explore which is, of course, one of the most important ways in which a child will learn. Older children will be striving for independence on a greater scale; they may wish to play at a friend's house for example or visit the park without an adult. It is essential that children are made aware of the dangers they face when they are out and about on their own and that they know how to handle themselves in an emergency. Remember, along with the child's parents, you need to be a positive role model that children will look up to and you need to make sure that you practise safe methods at all times during your working day.

Most people feel relaxed and 'safe' in their own homes however, children need to understand that most accidents actually happen in the home setting and therefore they need to be careful at all times. Young children for example may be confident climbing stairs however they need to understand the importance of how to come back down again safely if they are to master this feat of independence appropriately.

The definition of independence is being 'free from outside control or influence'. Allowing children independence means you are giving them the freedom and self-reliance to undertake an activity or enjoy an experience without intervention. You need to be completely sure that the child is old enough and responsible enough before allowing them this independence and that you seek written parental permission before allowing children in your care to go out alone.

Coping with new situations

Throughout their childhood, and indeed in later years, children will need to learn how to cope with and adapt to new situations. Some children may experience many more changes in their lives than others and childminders are often called upon to offer help and support when preparing children for these new situations. All children will, at some point, have to cope with starting school and the challenges they face can be daunting if the child is unprepared and therefore has difficulty adapting. Other changes that some children may experience include:

- The birth of a sibling
- The breakdown of their parents' relationship or marriage
- The death of a parent or close family member
- Moving house
- Moving school

Some children take change in their stride and can adapt easily while others are thrown completely off balance and may suffer immensely as a result. Many children rely on routine and knowing what to expect, to ensure that their day runs smoothly and they can be taken completely off guard by even the slightest of changes. Imagine then how they would feel if they moved house and left all their old friends behind to start school in a totally different area?

Divorce and separation are ultimately about change and a child's ability to accept these changes and cope with the 'loss' of one of their parents can be very difficult. As many as one in three marriages now ends in divorce and many of these involve families with children under the age of 5 years. Young children have little understanding of the emotional complexities involved in a marriage break-down and often feelings of anger, resentment, fear and anxiety will surface. The child's whole world as they know it, will fall apart and they may face a huge amount of upheaval and will inevitably be confused.

Another important milestone in a child's life, and one which may cause them some anxiety, is the arrival of a sibling. First-born children will have had time with their parents without the demands of any other children. These children will, in effect, face the hardest lesson of all – having to learn to share their parents! Having gone from being an only child to having to share their parents with a sibling can be unsettling for a child and add pressures and insecurity. Children will need patience and understanding while they are getting used to the situation.

It is important that childminders are aware of what is going on in a child's life if they are to effectively support and guide them through any difficult times they may be experiencing. Sometimes parents are reluctant to explain personal situations to an 'outsider' and this is a great shame. Childminders are often seen as a valued part of the family and as such are often trusted with a lot of sensitive information. If the parents feel assured that you will keep the information they share with you confidential and you are not the kind of person to judge and pass comment, then it should be much easier for them to open up and let you know of anything which may cause their child distress. You need to be aware of any major changes in a child's life in order that you can take into account any changes happening in the child's behaviour or demeanour. Always remember that during troubled, uncertain times you, the childminder, may be the only area of stability the child has in their life and they may depend heavily on your love, support and understanding.

5 Communication, Language and Literacy Development

This chapter directly relates to

- Unit 2 of the Diploma in Home-based Childcare: Childcare and Child Development (0–16) in the Home-based Setting
- The Learning and Development Requirements of The Early Years Foundation Stage

The early years are when the majority of children learn how to communicate through speech and often, during these early years, children learn how to speak in more than one language. However, it is important that childminders understand that spoken language is only a small part of communication and children learn to communicate in a variety of other ways such as gestures, facial expressions, body movements, signs etc.

How children develop communication and language skills

Imitation and reinforcement are perhaps the most widely used methods of encouraging a child to develop communication and language skills. Children love to imitate and, if they are rewarded with praise and encouragement, their interest becomes more intense. Child-minders should always make the time to praise a child who is learning to communicate through language and it is vital that they ensure that a child is never laughed at or ridiculed, even if this is in an affectionate way, if they have pronounced a word incorrectly or used it in the wrong context. How many of us have witnessed a child's embarrassment when they have had their mistakes highlighted? The result is usually that the child retreats into silence, and this is of course the very last thing we should be looking to encourage when helping a child develop their communication skills. Of course sometimes it is necessary to correct a child; perhaps for example, when they are trying to say a word for the first time and need reinforcement. Whenever possible, try to subtly rephrase the child's statement, while showing that you have understood them, rather than correcting grammatical mistakes. It is important to remember not to highlight every mis-pronunciation or grammatical error for fear of putting children off trying out new words and experimenting with language.

As children get a little older their need for imitation is coupled with their desire to think for themselves and grammatical errors will be made often. We know that the child is now thinking for themselves and applying certain rules they have learned as they now begin to say sentences they will not have heard before and are not therefore simply copying. For example a child may become confused when using tenses and use these in the wrong context or they may incorporate words of their own such as 'doed' instead of 'did', 'goed' instead of 'went' or 'worser' instead of worse.

Language for communication

Talking to children, even from being tiny babies, is absolutely essential. Children who hear lots of language are more likely to develop their own vocabulary at a greater rate. Talk to your baby, tell them what you are doing and describe things to them. Watch them as they observe you speaking to them and incorporate sounds as well as words. Very young babies will try to imitate the sounds and words you say and they can be quite comical when trying to shape their mouths to imitate the sounds they hear!

Children do not learn to speak in isolation and those who are deprived of adult interaction will not flourish with regard to their communication skills. Children do not need you to talk about in depth, complex issues and quite often they will engage in conversations regarding just about anything. In order to become a skilful communicator a child needs to be with adults they know and trust well in order for them to be given the time needed to communicate their feelings, ideas and thoughts effectively.

Exercise

Spend a couple of minutes sitting and listening to the children as they are playing. Listen to what they are saying, are they talking about anything in particular or are they muttering among themselves? Is the conversation aimed at anyone in particular? Do the children talk only about one topic or do they talk about several things during a short space of time?

When we think about using language we usually mean talking aloud and listening to what is being said. However the spoken word is, of course, not the only method of communicating through language. Sign language is also a way of communicating and where spoken language is not a successful method of communication, perhaps in the case of a person being deaf, then sign language may be the main method of communication practised. Other forms of communication may include:

- Body language – such as folded arms, pointed fingers, hands on hips etc.
- Eye contact
- Facial gestures – smiling, frowning, sulking etc.
- Hand gestures – waving, clapping etc.
- Writing
- Vocal noises – sighing, cooing, screaming etc.
- Reading

Children become more and more adept at communicating as they get older and they gradually increase their skills of using hand and facial gestures.

Language, and in particular the ability to communicate well, will affect almost all areas of a child's development – the exception being areas of physical development. Language is one of the main ways in which we are able to develop our thought processes, to reason, show expression, think and remember. Communication affects a child's:

- Emotional development
- Social development
- Cognitive development

Childminders can encourage a child's learning and competence in speaking and listening skills by engaging them often in conversation during everyday activities. By talking to the children and involving them in the things that you do such as cooking and preparing meals, setting the table and clearing away you will be continually encouraging their communication skills.

Language for thinking

By talking things through we are able to clarify our thoughts, work things out and understand concepts better. Developing the language for comparing and contrasting is the first basic tool for thinking and children need to be able to discriminate in order to build on their logical thought. Children need to be able to use language effectively in order to compare detail and childminders need to introduce words for comparison in every-day play and activities. Words such as 'bigger than', 'heavier than' and 'faster than' will encourage children to discriminate logically.

Language and thinking initially develop when the child responds to everything in the environment by using their senses. They should then be able to talk about their experiences knowing that they will be listened to and that they will have the opportunity to share their thoughts and ideas and have their questions answered.

Non-verbal communication

When we consider that approximately 95 per cent of communication is non-verbal we come to realize the importance of sharing conversations with children. Conversing is not the same as asking and giving specific questions and answers. Having a conversation means taking it in turns to say things which are relative to what we are thinking or feeling. Many young children find it difficult to wait their turn and waiting to speak is no exception.

As non-verbal communication forms a large part of conversing it is essential that children learn the importance of reading the facial expressions and gestures of others in order to be able to communicate effectively. Babies and young children are particularly adept at learning this skill and will recognize and respond to a smile from an adult. It is particularly important for children, who are exposed to more than one culture to be aware that facial expressions and gestures differ enormously.

Exercise

Make a list of all the ways we are able to communicate with each other apart from using the spoken word.

Reading

Young children get their first taste of reading when they become interested in listening to stories. Most children will enjoy listening to stories and these provide the child with the necessary tools to be able to read and write their own stories in later life. Stories can be either made up orally or read from a book and they may represent:

- Every-day life experiences and events
- Make believe
- Poems
- Action rhymes
- True stories

Sharing and enjoying stories with children is an excellent way of helping them to become competent readers as they can see how a book is used by the adult without need for any pressure on the child.

Reading is an essential skill which all children need to master. Once a child has mastered the spoken word, reading will be a natural progression for most children. In order to be able to read a child needs to understand that symbols have a meaning.

It is important, when encouraging children to read, that childminders understand how they can contribute to this aspect of learning. It is vital that your setting has a variety of books which are of interest to all the children. Think carefully about the age and stage of development of all of the children you care for and ensure that your books will engage the children's attention and imagination. Not all your books should be story books. A selection of reference books and books which encourage children to explore their own feelings and emotions are also essential as children need to learn that books can be a source of information as well as being entertaining.

Repetition is very important to young children who will often ask for a story to be read to them over and over again. When doing this, encourage the children to join in the story and, at appropriate times, ask them what they think will happen next as this will encourage the children to participate in the story and test their knowledge of what they have heard and understood. You could try introducing finger puppets and dolls to help illustrate the stories and encourage the children to take part.

Children need to learn how to handle books properly and with care. To begin with a child will turn the pages as a process of 'going through the motions' rather than because they are taking an interest in the actual words or pictures. Often the book will be upside down and the child will open it at the back and work forwards. Children need to be shown how to handle books with care and how to read from front to back. Show children the correct way of turning the pages over to prevent them from being torn and reiterate how important books are and why they should be handled correctly. Allow children to handle books; very young children should be provided with board books so that they can learn how to handle them correctly without fear of tearing the pages.

When you are reading to children it is a good idea to get into the habit of following these points in order to encourage them to read and promote an interest in books and stories:

- Encourage the children to look at the pictures carefully.
- Invite the children to say what they think is happening by using the pictures as a reference.
- Read the text slowly and clearly.
- Point to the words as you read them to allow the children the chance to recognize that you are saying what you see.
- Point out any rhyming patterns in the text.
- Encourage the children to repeat the words.
- Let the children see your own enthusiasm for books and explain to them how books can be a wonderful source of information.
- Provide a variety of books in several different languages which reflect the interests and abilities of all of the children in your setting.

It is important to be aware of the four 'aspects of print'. These aspects are:

- The *semantic* aspect – this is the *meaning* of the print.
- The *grammar* aspect – this is the *flow* of the print.
- The *graphophonic* aspect – this is the *look* (grapho) and *sound* (phonic) of the text.
- The *vocabulary* aspect – this is the *language* of the book.

Most schools today emphasize all aspects of print when teaching children how to read. Always try to point out the words as you read them so that children are encouraged to make sense of print. A good starting point, when teaching children to read, is to get them to recognize their own name. This can be particularly useful as children are emotionally attached to their name and will be interested in learning to read words which are personal to them.

It is important to remember that all children begin to read by using the pictures in the book to 'guess' the story line and this should be encouraged where possible.

Writing

As with reading, writing also has 'aspects'. The two aspects to writing are:

- The construction of meaning – what the writing actually says and
- The transcription of the handwriting – what the writing actually looks like.

Children will begin to 'write' by introducing letter type 'shapes' to their drawings. These shapes will be personal to each individual child and may not look like any type of conventional writing. The script may begin as scribble and, after being allowed to experiment, the child will master how to make shapes in varying sizes. It is important that children are allowed to experiment in this way before any adult interference is introduced in order to allow them to try out different ways of 'writing' which are personal to them. A child who shows a preference in writing using their left hand should never be discouraged from doing so and resources for left-handed people should be provided where necessary.

Childminders can actively help and encourage the children in their care and promote their writing skills by:

- Supplying the children with a wide range of tools for mark making and writing including pens, pencils, crayons etc.
- Encouraging children to experiment with other forms of writing such as typing, using computers, emails and text.
- Encouraging the children to write their own name and praising their efforts for all writing practice.
- Encouraging children to write letters and make notes.

Multilingual children

If you are caring for a child who is learning more than one language you may have noticed that their speech and communication development is slightly slower than children who are only learning to grasp one language. This is perfectly normal and the delay should not affect the child's overall language development.

A child who is learning more than one language may however require additional support in order for them to absorb and respond to each of the different languages they hear. Children who are unfamiliar with a language will pass through a phase of becoming silent when they are absorbing what they are hearing around them. This means that a child may be hearing English and understanding the structure of grammar, however they are not yet confident to speak the language. If you yourself have ever learnt a second language you will probably remember that it is easier to understand what is being said than it is to actually construct your own sentences. This particular stage of a child's development may last months

and sometimes years and the child will most definitely require support. This silent period is not a time for the child to be left alone and they should be encouraged to take part and for the childminder to talk and listen to the child and involve them in all activities.

Children will become competent at speaking and 'matching' the appropriate language to the correct environment and they should not be 'put on show' or made an example of in the childminding setting. Do not be tempted to encourage a multilingual child to show off his skills by asking him to say certain words in his home language as this may embarrass him in front of his peers or put pressure on him to 'perform' for others. In this kind of situation children can often become confused and may even struggle to find the words requested of them which will result in them feeling inadequate in both languages. Children will quickly become adept at speaking the correct language depending on the environment they are in and will soon learn to speak their first language at home and English when in the childminding setting. It is always a good idea to learn one or two important phrases from the first language of any children you are caring for, and where appropriate, these words and phrases could be taught to the other children in order to make all the children feel welcome and valued. If it helps you to pronounce the words correctly try writing them down phonetically. You should also make sure that you provide books in all the languages the children in your setting speak and ensure that labels, signs, posters and displays reflect a variety of languages. It is absolutely vital that a child's home language is recognized and valued in order for the child to feel welcome in the childminding setting. A child's first language is part of their identity and as such it needs to be recognized and understood. Childminders need to create an atmosphere in their setting where *all* children, regardless of the languages they speak, feel comfortable and able to play, learn and participate as equals in the activities on offer. It is important to understand that children who are multilingual may have emotional and social needs in addition to other needs connected with their language development such as:

- **Embarrassment:** Never ask a child to demonstrate their language skills, unless they are happy to do so, as this can often become a burden to the child and cause embarrassment. Children rarely wish to be different from their peers and to prevent such feelings they may even pretend that they do not speak another language.
- **Rejection:** This is a form of racism when children may feel that their home language along with their culture is not valued and therefore is unimportant. They may fear rejection if they seem in anyway different from their peers.

It is very important that childminders are sensitive to the needs of multilingual children and this can be done by building up a good relationship with the child and their family and by showing them that they are valued in the setting. Encourage the parents of the child to become involved, ask their opinions and request their input when promoting different language development within the childminding setting.

Factors affecting language and communication

There could be a number of reasons why a child's language and communication skills may be delayed and it is important that childminders are aware of the factors which may affect a child's communication in order to avoid behavioural difficulties such as the child becoming clingy or aggressive as a result of not being understood. Factors which may affect a child's language and communication skills include:

- Hearing impairments
- Physical conditions
- Learning difficulties
- Multilingual communication
- Shyness
- Stuttering or stammering

Hearing impairments

Hearing impairments may be temporary for example as the result of a particularly bad cold or glue ear, or they may be permanent in the case of a child who is either fully or partially deaf. Hearing difficulties are a common reason for a child's delayed language development and it is important that you are aware of the signs exhibited if a child is having difficulty hearing. These signs may include:

- Appearing to ignore questions or requests.
- Showing a lack of response if their name is called.
- Appearing to show little interest in activities.
- Continually looking at the mouths of those who are speaking in order to make out the words being spoken.
- Often mispronouncing words or names.

If you feel that a child in your setting is showing any of the above signs it is important that you mention your concerns to the child's parent so that you can monitor the child together and seek professional help if necessary.

Physical conditions

A child may have a physical condition such as a cleft palate or an enlarged tongue which may result in delayed language development. In these cases, depending on the severity of the child's physical condition, it may be necessary for you to work with other professionals and the child's parents in order to help and encourage the child's communication. Sensitivity is paramount at all times as is a flexible, calm and patient approach to the child's learning and development.

Learning difficulties

Children with learning difficulties such as autism may often become angry and frustrated due to their difficulty in communication and, once again, the childminder will need to show a calm and patient approach. You will need to show added understanding and reassure the child often if they have problems making themselves understood. Often professional help will be required to help the communication of children with learning difficulties.

Multilingual communication

As we have mentioned previously a child who speaks more than one language may have a communication delay as they struggle to grasp two languages. This kind of developmental delay will rarely affect the child's overall development although they may need additional support initially.

Shyness

A shy child, who is lacking in confidence and self-esteem, may have difficulty communicating as they struggle to overcome their feelings of self-doubt. Shy children will often prefer to 'dissolve' into the background and will find it difficult to take part in group sessions. You will need to build the child's self-esteem in order to boost their confidence and show patience and understanding in abundance.

Stuttering or stammering

Stuttering and stammering is very common in young children and is often a result of their minds working faster than their tongues. They may know exactly what they wish to say but their mouths have difficulty expressing their thoughts at the same speed! Couple this with a fear that another child may interrupt what they wish to say and the overall 'rush' to speak results in a stuttering or stammering child. Most often the child will grow out of this phase however, for some children, the stutter or stammer will become a habit and therefore much harder to drop and in these cases it may be necessary to involve a speech therapist for expert advice. There are several ways in which childminders can help a child who is showing signs of stuttering or stammering and these include:

- Encouraging the child to slow down and to speak slowly.
- Reassuring the child that no one will be allowed to interrupt them.
- Ensuring that the child has your undivided attention and that they are aware of this.
- Avoiding rushing the child.
- Avoiding finishing the child's sentences for them.
- Making good eye contact with the child.
- Aiming to get the child to relax before they begin to speak.

Problem Solving, Reasoning and Numeracy   6

This chapter directly relates to

- Unit 2 of the Diploma in Home-based Childcare: Childcare and Child Development (0–16) in the Home-based Setting
- The Learning and Development Requirements of The Early Years Foundation Stage

It is important that childminders understand the importance of allowing the children in their care the time and space required to enable them to discover and understand mathematical ideas, concepts and language.

Childminders need to encourage and support children as well as provide them with opportunities to practise their skills in order for them to gain confidence.

Numbers for counting

Children learn to count in early mathematics by putting into practice some important concepts. These concepts are:

- Reciting numbers in order, for example counting out loud from one to ten, perhaps when climbing stairs or playing a game.
- Being able to count objects correctly by saying one number at a time while touching the objects being counted.

- Being able to separate certain objects which have been counted from those which have not been counted.
- Being able to mentally recognize how many objects are in a small group without the need to touch each object individually to count them.

It can be difficult for children to understand that moving objects around, but not taking any away, does not affect the amount. Most young children, if interrupted when counting, will begin again and start counting each object rather than carry on from where they left off. As a child becomes more adept at their counting skills they will learn to understand the real meaning of counting and that is to find out how many objects there are. To begin with children will be inclined to line objects up in a row before beginning to count them; this obviously makes the task easier for the child as they can easily see which objects have been counted and which have not. However, as their counting skills progress they will recognize that it doesn't matter which order the objects are counted in or whether they are in a line or randomly arranged. In time children will master how to self-check when counting and will rely less and less on having to touch the objects they are counting.

It is important that we reiterate why it is necessary to count in order for children to understand the importance of mastering this essential skill and childminders can encourage children to practise counting regularly such as at meal times when it is possible to encourage the children to add up how many place settings are needed for lunch, how many knives, forks and spoons are required. Encourage the children to count when tidying the toys away and explain how, when counting, it is possible to see if there are any pieces missing from the jigsaw puzzle or whether all the building bricks have been picked up and placed back in the box.

There are many aids available to encourage children to count and childminders need to consider which resources will be useful for the ages and stages of development of the children they are caring for. Younger children for example can be encouraged to count with the use of building bricks to make towers or large counters in various colours which can be sorted into groups and counted. Older children can be encouraged to thread beads onto a string and count how many are needed to make a necklace or bracelet. Games of snakes and ladders and dominoes are also excellent ways of encouraging children to count and recognize number sequences.

Calculating

In recent years researchers have discovered that children are natural problem solvers and do not, as previously thought, resort to trial and error in order to solve a problem. We now know that even young babies are capable of making a 'hypothesis'. Making a hypothesis means developing a theory which can be tested to see if it is correct. Although many young children under the age of 2 often make an incorrect hypothesis experts believe that this is a very important part of the child's development of problem solving.

A young child often begins to develop their knowledge of calculation through addition and subtraction activities in everyday life. Everyday play experiences provide a wide range of opportunities for children to learn to count and it is through these experiences that they will gain more of an understanding of calculation. Children can be encouraged to learn about calculation by introducing simple problems for them to solve. Try placing a row of five bricks in front of the child and, asking them to calculate how many bricks are in the row after you have added one or taken one away.

Introducing words such as 'more' and 'less' will help to reinforce language used in communication and encourage the children to develop their own understanding of the language of calculation.

There are a number of other important words and phrases associated with number and calculation which children should be encouraged to add to their vocabulary. Childminders can help the children they care for to become familiar with these words and phrases by using them often themselves. These words include:

- Numbers from zero through to ten
- More than, less than
- Fewer
- None
- How many?
- Share out
- How much?
- Least

- Most
- The same as
- Nearly
- Compare
- Difference
- Altogether

Shape, space and measures

In our everyday lives we come across many shapes which are often impossible to describe. For example the shape of a kettle which is sort of cylindrical or a flight of stairs which can be either curved or straight with varying angles. However some shapes do have specific names and it is important that children are encouraged to recognize these shapes. Children need to be aware of the differences between shapes and childminders need to provide the children in their care with both 2D and 3D shapes so that the children can look closely at the faces of a solid object and compare these to flat shapes. Children will only get a real understanding of the properties of shapes if they are allowed to investigate them and have the opportunity to handle shapes made of different materials and of varying size.

It is important that young children are not bombarded with too many technical terms when encouraging them to learn about shape and size as this may overwhelm and confuse them. Although children need to learn the names of shapes it is far better for the childminder to gradually introduce these and they should begin by using general terms to help the children in their care to learn about mathematical aspects. There are dozens of opportunities for childminders to talk about shape and size while going about their every-day tasks and they should be using these opportunities to talk to the children. You should be talking about how things are 'bigger' or 'small', 'heavier' or 'lighter', 'fatter' or 'thinner' at every opportunity. Simple tasks such as peeling and slicing fruit can be turned into a mathematical experience with the children if you encourage them to say which fruit is the heaviest, which is the smallest, which is round etc. Objects such as tins can be described as being cylindrical and a ball as a sphere.

Shape and size can be split into four separate categories and these are:

- Length
- Weight
- Area
- Volume and capacity

Length

Young children will have difficulty recognizing absolute concepts such as metre, centimetre, millimetre etc., and it is therefore important to use relative terms when describing length.

By asking questions such as 'Do you think the banana is longer than the carrot?' rather than 'how long do you think the banana is?' will help children to compare two objects and determine which is the longest rather than confusing them by asking for specific lengths. Likewise, comparisons can be made when building towers from bricks, children will be able to determine which tower is the longest and which is the shortest. Once this concept has been grasped they can then be encouraged to calculate the difference in the height of each tower by adding up how many bricks the tallest is and subtracting the amount of the bricks the shortest is made up of.

Weight

Once again young children will have difficulty recognizing absolute concepts and you will need to introduce relative ideas such as asking if the apple is heavier than the melon. Weighing scales can be introduced at a later stage once the child has mastered the basic differences in weight.

Area

Area can be a difficult concept for young children to grasp and it is best to use ideas that they can actually see when introducing this mathematical term. For example a rug covers a certain area of the floor; the butter covers the area of the slice of bread.

Volume and capacity

Young children may struggle to see volume and capacity in specific measurements such as cubic litres, pints etc., however they will be able to explore the concept of volume and capacity by being allowed to play in water and experiment using a variety of containers. The cup is half full, the jug is over flowing, the bucket is almost full to the top are all mathematical expressions which young children will be able to relate to.

Some important words and phrases which are associated with shape, space and measures, which children should be encouraged to add to their vocabulary include:

- Bigger, larger
- Smaller
- Guess
- Compare
- Enough
- Too much, too little
- Length, width and height
- Long, longer and longest
- Short, shorter and shortest
- Tall, taller and tallest
- Low, lower and lowest
- Wide, wider and widest
- Narrow, narrower and narrowest
- Thick and thin

Developing attention span and memory

Memory and attention are fundamental components of how children learn. Memory is made up of two areas, short-term memory and long-term memory.

Short-term memory

It is thought that the average human brain can store information in their short-term memory for between 15 and 30 seconds before it is discarded. We use our short-term memory to store information which is only required in the interim and which, once used, can then be forgotten. It is possible to increase the length of time we are able to store information in our short-term memory by reciting it over and over again. For example, if we need to remember an address it is possible, by repeating it many times, that we will be able to store it, for some time, in our short-term memory. Young children however do not have the ability to do this and as such they often forget simple instructions or information they have just been told.

Long-term memory

The capacity of our long-term memory is vast. We use our long-term memory to store a huge amount of information which is not necessarily needed immediately. Our long-term memory gives us the ability to retrieve data as and when it is required. Although sometimes it may not be possible to remember all that is required our memories will allow us to come to the correct solution through a process of elimination. For example we may not be able to recall exact names of people or places however we can often determine whether a suggested one is correct or incorrect.

It is important that children are encouraged to develop memory skills and build on their attention span in order to be able to learn new skills and knowledge. Without the ability to concentrate for periods of time a child will have difficulty storing information long enough to process it and will ultimately be unable to learn from their experiences or develop their knowledge. Childminders therefore need to be able to encourage the children in their care to remember events, activities and experiences and this can be done by gentle questioning to encourage the development of the memory span. The brain uses attention and concentration skills to filter out distractions going on around us so that we are able to focus on the job in hand. This does not of course mean that we are unable to direct our attention to more than one task at once and multitasking is something which comes with practice as the child gets older, however it is necessary for a child to be able to filter out distractions such as noise, smells and other interruptions in order for them to be able to focus on set tasks or activities. An inability to do this will result in the child flitting from one activity to another without ever finishing anything.

Exercise

Why do you think some children find it difficult to pay attention and focus on one particular activity for a reasonable length of time? Are there any children in your care who you consider to have a short attention span? If so, why do you think this is the case? Spend some time observing the child. How long do they appear to concentrate before they are distracted? What appears to distract them? How can you make sure that distractions are kept to a minimum in order to encourage the child to concentrate on the task in hand?

7 Knowledge and Understanding of the World

This chapter directly relates to

- Unit 2 of the Diploma in Home-based Childcare: Childcare and Child Development (0–16) in the Home-based Setting
- The Learning and Development Requirements of The Early Years Foundation Stage

Childminders need to support children in developing the knowledge, skills and understanding that are required in order for them to make sense of the world in which we live. In order for children to learn successfully about the world it is necessary for them to have the opportunity to use a range of tools safely and to be able to explore and investigate their natural environment while taking part in real-life experiences.

Exploration and investigation

Children love to explore and it is necessary, in order for them to gain the skills needed to develop an understanding of the environment, for them to be allowed to explore and investigate safely. It is now widely accepted that children learn much more by *doing* rather than simply *observing* and it is therefore essential that childminders provide the children in their care with the opportunities to take part in 'hands on' experiences and to witness for themselves first hand what something feels like rather than to simply watch what an adult is doing. Participation is an important part of a child's learning and all children need the opportunity to explore and investigate things for themselves.

One of the most beneficial, and easiest, ways of encouraging children to explore and investigate is to make the most of spontaneous events such as using a sudden downpour of rain to investigate rainbows or a flurry of snow to explore ice patterns, introduce climate changes and to look at how water changes under extreme temperatures. Children will be able to relate to and understand these concepts if they are allowed to put on Wellington boots and coats and go outside to experience the snow, ice and rain first hand rather than resorting to the childminder describing these events for them or having to rely on pictures in a book. Simple tasks such as jumping in a puddle or making a snowman engage children in exploration and investigation of their environment. In much the same way a child who has never been to the seaside will have difficulty relating to how the sand feels between their toes by listening to an adult describe this feeling however, by providing a sand pit or emptying a bag of sand onto a polythene mat and encouraging the child to witness first hand how the sand feels they will learn much more by being allowed to experience the sensation for themselves.

Outdoor play is essential and the minds and bodies of young children will develop and thrive when they have free access to fresh air and outdoor exercise which provides stimulating play and real-life experiences.

Children also need to be able to explore and investigate plants, creatures, people and objects in order to understand the natural environment and it is the job of the childminder to offer a range of activities and experiences which will encourage children's interest and curiosity both indoors and outdoors.

Exercise

Think about the many ways in which children explore and investigate the world around them. Spend some time observing the children in your care. How does the exploration of a baby differ to that of a child of 3 years of age?

Designing and making

Children need to be allowed to design and make objects using a variety of materials which are both natural and manmade. They need to be encouraged to take part in modelling and construction activities and should be provided with materials which are appropriate for their age and stage of development.

It is very important that children are allowed a 'hands on' approach and that they are encouraged to take their own initiative when it comes to designing and making rather than being told to copy something an adult has made. Children need to be able to follow their own preferences and use their own design ideas and the emphasis should be on the actual process of the design rather than the end product. While a child's design may appear ineffective it

is important for the childminder to realize that the actual process of designing rather than the finished product may be encouraging discovery and the children can learn a great deal by putting their ideas into practice in this way.

One of the easiest and cheapest ways for a childminder to encourage the children in their care to use designing and making to help them with their knowledge and understanding of the world is to provide a range of 'junk' for them to work with and for them to adapt the junk to make a wide range of objects. It may be necessary to offer children a fairly limited range of materials initially so as not to overwhelm them however, you should then gradually introduce more and more choice and variety and encourage the children to choose the materials they wish to use depending on what they are hoping to make and the particular technique they intend to practise.

Design and technology is all about finding out about how the world was made and understanding how it works and what we can do to change or modify it. By providing children with a variety of materials to work with we are encouraging them to find out about different properties such as how they can be managed, whether they are rigid or pliable, whether they are waterproof or porous or whether they are strong or weak. We can encourage them to experiment with different ways of joining materials together and to see whether glue, paste or tape has sufficient bonding capacity. Knowing how materials can be utilized can only come about from being allowed to handle them, play about with them and experiment with them and this needs to be done through first hand experience for children to understand for themselves rather than being imagined or told.

Designing and making shouldn't simply be looked at as a way of making things as, quite often, much can be learnt by taking things apart! Radios, torches and watches are useful everyday objects which hold an endless fascination for young children and, if they are allowed to take these objects apart to learn how they work they may be able to incorporate what they have discovered in their own model making and construction designs.

Exercise

Look at the resources in your own setting. Do you have sufficient resources to encourage a child's designing and making potential? What items do you consider you could add to your existing resources which would extend this activity?

ICT

Information and communication technology is an essential part of all of our everyday lives and children are no exception. How much high-tech equipment you provide for the children in your care will depend very much on the amount of money you have in your budget, however there are a number of items of equipment, other than expensive computers, which are cheap and easily obtainable and which will provide children with the opportunity to explore this kind of technology such as:

- Television
- Video/DVD
- CD
- Tape recorder
- Programmable toys
- Radio

Technology touches almost every aspect of our everyday lives and it is important to remember that today's young children do not know life without aeroplanes, television, internet access, email and credit cards. Our lives have changed dramatically over recent years because of the increase in technology and, in an ever advancing world, it is important for children to learn how machines work and to understand the advantages they offer us. Children need to know how to find their way around a keyboard and how to use a mouse. If your budget doesn't stretch to a computer or laptop then think of alternative ways of introducing technology to your setting in order for the children to experiment with and explore.

Programmable toys are widely available and relatively cheap and they are a fantastic way of introducing young children to the world of technology as the toy allows the child to give instructions such as forward, back, right or left and this encourages the child to develop logical thinking, spatial awareness and sequencing.

CD-ROMs can open up a whole world of exploration for a child and allow them to be able to explore a vast number of areas such as under water, outer space, other countries etc., and the potential for a child to experience other environments, sounds and sights is huge.

One of the major areas of ICT is the handling of information and this is all about seizing, storing, searching and using information. In order to become efficient in these areas of handling information it is necessary for children to master how to:

- Sort, classify and organize data successfully.
- Utilize the information stored in order to find out the answers to their questions.
- Analyse data in the form of graphs and charts.
- Present their findings suitably.
- Make predictions and hypothesis.

The internet is a wonderful resource and can open up a whole new world of fascination and learning for children. Thousands of websites dedicated to a huge array of topics can be accessed at the touch of a button. ICT is a versatile teaching and learning tool that can be used in many ways to support children's learning. It can be particularly useful for children who may have problems accessing the curriculum due to learning difficulties or hearing, visual, emotional or behavioural problems as the wealth of software available, which is designed to support children with special educational needs, is diverse.

> **Exercise**
>
> How do you incorporate ICT into your setting? Do you consider your own resources for promoting this area of learning as being adequate? If not, what do you consider you can do to improve your ICT facilities?

Time

Time is a difficult concept for young children to understand quite simply because time cannot be 'seen'. In order for children to grasp the idea of time it is necessary to put it into context. For example, while most children can remember what they did an hour ago they may have trouble remembering what they did last week, last month or during the summer holidays. They can look forward to events but have little understanding of the passage of time and, if told that their birthday is next week they will probably be unable to ascertain exactly how long away it is. Often young children will work out how many 'sleeps' there are before an actual day arrives as they are then able to put time into context.

It is a good idea to talk to the children about the sequence of the week and encourage them to remember which days follow on from each other and what they can expect to happen on certain days of the week for example you may have a regular trip to the library on Monday, a trip to the local toddler group on Tuesday and attend the play gym on Friday. By encouraging the children to remember the first hand experiences they enjoy on each day you can help them to recognize the sequence of the days of the week.

In order to help children to understand the concept of time more easily it is a good idea to think about introducing history to the setting. Photographs are particularly helpful for encouraging children to understand how things and people have changed over periods of time and most children are fascinated by old photographs. The use of diaries to record special occasions, are a good way of introducing time to young children.

Childminders need to introduce words associated with time to the children's vocabulary to encourage them to understand the concept of the passing of time and these words include:

- Hour, minute and second
- Day, week, month and year
- Yesterday, tomorrow and today

Place

Children need to get to know their environment in order for them to begin to develop the skills required for geographical exploration and it is the job of the childminder to encourage the children in their care to explore their immediate surroundings using all of their senses. A child who is new to the setting will not initially know where things are stored and they will need to be encouraged to find their way around your home and garden before learning where the toys and equipment are stored and what kind of daily routine they can expect.

In addition to knowing where things are kept within the setting children should be encouraged to learn about their local environment and this might include looking at how buildings have been constructed, which materials have been used, what the buildings are used for and who works in them.

Children can be encouraged to develop a sense of space by introducing simple maps. These could be home made or simple street maps which can be used when out and about to enable the children to get a feel for the area they live in and become familiar with their local community. By encouraging young children to develop early map work skills you can also help them to focus on concepts of direction and location.

Childminders can reiterate the importance of 'place' by telling the children stories about places and journeys.

Communities

It is very important that children learn about the community they live in and that they feel part of it. Not all children will attend a childminding setting or school in the area where they live and it is therefore important that childminders understand the necessity of involving children in the community and making the most of any opportunities which arise enabling them to investigate their environment, first hand. Children need to be allowed to make effective use of their community as a resource for learning and it is important that they are encouraged to learn about both the differences and the similarities between features, landmarks and places within their immediate locality.

When encouraging children to learn about their community it is possible to extend their learning and encourage them to develop positive attitudes towards other people and to embrace different races, religions, colour, gender and ability. It may be relatively easy, in some areas, for children to have the opportunity to mix and socialize with others from a variety of diverse backgrounds however, as this is not always possible, childminders need to ensure that they provide the children in their care with positive attitudes in order for them to integrate in the diverse community we now live in.

Dressing up and role play provide ideal opportunities for children to explore a range of clothes worn by different people in the community and provide them with a way to explore the jobs these people do. It also encourages children to develop an empathy for their own environment and those individuals who live and work within it.

Physical Development and Well-being

Chapter Outline

This chapter directly relates to

- Unit 2 of the Diploma in Home-based Childcare: Childcare and Child Development (0–16) in the Home-based Setting
- The Learning and Development Requirements of The Early Years Foundation Stage

All babies and children will follow a standard, basic pattern when they are acquiring physical skills, however these patterns will vary enormously from individual to individual. A child's acquisition of new physical skills will have a huge impact on their lives; for example they will become more independent as they learn new skills, perhaps as a result of being able to crawl or walk, they will provoke different responses in those around them and the adults who care for them will make allowances for the child's new found skills.

Growth

Growth is closely linked with physical development and it is impossible for a child to achieve certain areas of physical development until their body has grown and matured accordingly. For example, a child will be unable to stand and walk until their bones have grown long enough and strong enough to support the child's weight. The whole process of growth will result in changes to the shape of a child's body and, at times, parents and carers may notice how a child seems to have grown rapidly in one area and not in others. The head of a baby, for example, makes up approximately a quarter of their overall height at birth, however by the time the child reaches maturity the body will have grown in other areas until the head makes up only approximately an eighth of the overall height of the person.

Once a baby is born their growth is monitored by weighing and measuring them and this is done in three ways:

- Weight of body
- Height of body
- Head circumference

The results of the above measurements are usually recorded on a percentile chart by health visitors or doctors.

Growth refers to an increase in physical size. While growth is measured in the ways listed above it is determined by four factors these being:

- Hormones
- Heredity
- Nutrition
- Emotions

Height and weight

Children will inherit genes and chromosomes from their parents which will make the basis of controlling the child's height.

It is very important that childminders are aware of how a child grows and develops in order for them to ensure that the child is progressing successfully. Although there are certain guidelines which we must be aware of it is also vital that we remember that all children are unique and while they may progress rapidly in some areas of growth they may also be slow to develop in others. Growth in height is usually determined by four phases and these are:

- Phase 1 – in the first 2 years of life a baby will usually grow rapidly.
- Phase 2 – from the age of 2 years through to adolescence, growth has usually slowed down and the child is now growing at a more steady rate.

- Phase 3 – when a child reaches adolescence they usually experience a rapid growth spurt.
- Phase 4 – growth has slowed down once again during this phase when only small increases in height and weight are made. By the time a person reaches the age of 18–20 years they are usually at their final adult size.

Exercise

Compare the size and weight of the children in your care. Do some children differ in height and weight considerably despite being of the same age? Do some children appear to grow more rapidly than others?

Gross motor skills

The term 'gross motor skills' covers the body's ability to make large movements such as jumping, running, walking, climbing and crawling. Gross motor skills require whole limb movements in order for the child to achieve the desired skill.

By the time a child reaches the age of 5 years they should have mastered a wide range of gross motor skills and should be showing increased agility. They should be able to run, dodge, climb and skip and be able to balance on 1 foot for about 10 seconds. As the child gets older they will gain in both strength and agility and their development of gross motor skills will develop as a result.

Fine motor skills

The term 'fine motor skills' covers the body's ability to make small movements such as grasping, squeezing and kneading; fine motor skills are required for the child to be able to manipulate objects for example holding a pencil to write or draw is termed as a fine motor skill, so too is adding a building block to a tower.

The development of fine motor skills will vary enormously between young children and while some 3-year-old children may be competent at doing up buttons or tying shoelaces others may be 5 or 6 years of age before they can master these particular fine motor skills.

Coordination

Although we have looked at the importance of gross and fine motor skills it is essential that we understand the importance of coordination as this is needed to carry out all activities. The most specific types of coordination, which are necessary for development include:

- Hand–eye coordination
- Balance
- Foot–eye coordination

Hand–eye coordination

Some activities require the eye to guide the hands. For example throwing and catching a ball and writing or drawing are all skills which require the eye to coordinate the hands in order to master the skill. In order to be able to carry out these tasks a child will need to use their eyes to receive information which they then use to coordinate their hands.

Balance

Balance is not an easy task for young children to master and this is something that comes with age. Balance is controlled by the central nervous system and it is the ability to coordinate information received from it. Balance is required to sit, stand and walk before other tasks are learned such as turning, twisting and bending.

Foot–eye coordination

As with hand–eye coordination some activities such as kicking a ball, climbing stairs, running and skipping with a rope will require the eye to receive information to guide the feet.

The speed at which a child will carry out some of these tasks will come with practice and their ability to guide their feet successfully based on what they can see.

Exercise

Think about the following skills and decide whether they require fine motor skills, gross motor skills, coordination or a mixture in order for the child to successfully carry them out:

- Put beads into a small container
- Squat to look closely at toys
- Take off and put on shoes
- Build a tower from blocks
- Use a spoon to feed themselves
- Hit a ball with a bat
- Turn the pages of a book
- Put together a jigsaw puzzle
- Climb on furniture

Movement and space

Childminders need to be aware that they have a responsibility to encourage the children in their care to develop their physical skills and awareness through the provision of opportunities which will allow the child to improve and develop their skills of coordination, control, manipulation and movement.

Movement and space involves a child being able to:

- Move with confidence
- Move with imagination
- Move in safety
- Move with control and coordination
- Be able to show an awareness of space both for themselves and for others
- Travel around, under, over and through equipment

Childminders need to learn how to use the space available in their homes and gardens to enable children to explore and make the most of movement. You need to think carefully about the setup of your indoor and outdoor areas and ensure that your furniture and equipment is organized in a way that enables children to run, hop, jump, dance, climb, balance and explore their environment while being aware of safety issues and having consideration for others.

Using equipment and materials

In order to encourage the physical development of children it is important that childminders understand how to provide appropriate equipment and materials to encourage their control and manipulation.

Props and toys are essential for children to play with. Often children will adapt the toys and materials on offer and make their own props. It is not important to provide expensive toys and equipment and it is often the items which are inexpensive or free which provide the most imaginative and interactive play opportunities. In order to be able to supply children with the appropriate equipment and materials needed for them to explore and develop their abilities we need to look at the different areas of child development, and which areas of their development we are hoping to extend.

For example social and emotional play may take into account communication development and puppets, books, musical instruments and games would all be successful at promoting this. Likewise physical play which takes into account gross and fine motor skills could be promoted with the use of building bricks, climbing apparatus, dance and music.

Exercise

Think of the different areas of child development we have looked at in this book and make a list of appropriate equipment and materials which you could provide to promote each of these developmental areas.

Health and bodily awareness

Health and bodily awareness is all about helping children to understand the importance of keeping healthy and learning about how they can achieve this. Children need to be aware of the changes which occur within their bodies when they are active and understand the importance of physical activity and healthy food choices.

Childminders need to ensure that they provide the children in their care with daily opportunities to develop their physical skills and they need to ensure that they offer them a healthy balanced diet.

Exercise

It is probably true to say that some children will have little opportunity to take part in daily exercise other than when they are at school. This may be due to the child's family attitudes and habits. Whereas once the majority of children walked to and from school nowadays they are much more likely to travel to school in a car which, once again deprives them of the everyday physical exercise that, in the past, most children took for granted. It is therefore essential that childminders ensure that the children they are caring for are given ample opportunity to exercise every day to ensure that they develop their motor skills and are given the opportunity to release pent-up frustration and energy.

It is a known fact that exercise is crucial to our well-being and, adults who are physically inactive have an increased chance of suffering from coronary heart disease. It goes without saying therefore that the importance of daily exercise needs to be instilled in children as early as possible in order for them to grow up with the knowledge of the importance of physical exercise so that they see exercise as a way of life rather than a necessary chore.

Children need to be aware of how their bodies respond to daily exercise and this can be done by asking the children to describe how they feel both before and after a physical exercise session. They need to be aware of the changes that happen to their bodies when they are active such as the increase in their heartbeat and pulse and how their breathing is affected, all of which come about after physical exercise. It is paramount however that childminders ensure that all physical exercise is done in a fun and interesting way which engages the imagination of the child to ensure that they remain committed to keeping their bodies healthy.

Diet

A healthy, balanced diet, coupled with daily physical exercise, is crucial to the development of children. It is not simply sufficient to serve healthy meals and snacks; it is vital that children understand the importance of eating a healthy balanced diet so that they themselves are more likely to choose healthy options when given a choice.

Diet is all about educating the individual to understand the importance of eating sensibly while understanding that they can enjoy food. Food habits are developed during childhood which will affect us for all of our lives and this is why it is important for children to develop healthy eating habits from the outset. Establishing healthy eating habits in the early years will encourage children to eat sensibly throughout their lives, promote normal growth and development and protect against disease in later life.

There are five main groups of foods which all provide essential nutrients. Foods from each of these groups should be provided on a daily basis in order to ensure a balanced, healthy diet. These food groups are:

- Potatoes and cereals
- Fruit and vegetables
- Milk and milk products
- Foods high in protein
- Fats and oils

Let us now look at each food group in more detail:

Potatoes and cereals These foods are high in energy and they contain both vitamins and minerals. Some of the foods which can be found in this group include bread, potatoes, pasta, rice and breakfast cereals. In order to achieve a healthy, balanced diet children require five servings per day from this food group. A serving may consist of a potato, a slice of bread, a portion of pasta or a bowl of breakfast cereal.

Fruit and vegetables These foods are full of vitamins, minerals and fibre and are essential for good health. Children should be given four servings from this food group per day. A serving may consist of a portion of vegetables, a glass of fruit juice, a piece of fruit or a portion of dried fruit such as raisins or sultanas. It is important to remember that raw fruit and vegetables are a more healthy option than cooked fruit and vegetables as their vitamin content may be destroyed in the cooking process therefore, wherever possible, try to encourage children to eat raw vegetables such as carrot and celery sticks.

Milk and milk products These foods contain calcium. Children need a pint of milk per day in order to ensure their essential intake of calcium. Calcium can also be derived from cheese and yoghurts. Children should be given three servings from this food group per day. A serving may consist of a glass of milk, a yoghurt, a fromage frais or a portion of cheese perhaps grated in a sandwich or served as cheese on toast.

Foods high in protein The foods which are high in protein include lean meat, fish, poultry, eggs, tofu and quorn and pulses. Children should be given two servings from this food group per day. A serving may consist of a portion of baked beans, a portion of lentils, fish fingers, scrambled egg or a piece of chicken.

Fats and oils Fats and oils are derived from all of the foods in the four groups mentioned above. For example fats will be obtained from cheese and meat and oil can be derived from some vegetables. Each of the foods from these four food groups will provide sufficient fats and oils if consumed on a daily basis.

Other foods, which although high energy foods, contain excessive amounts of sugar and have little or no nutritional value, include sweets, cakes, crisps and chocolate. These foods are likely to boost energy levels in the short term but can lead to sugar cravings and run the risk of excessive weight gain and tooth decay if eaten in excess. There is no reason why these kinds of foods cannot be offered as occasional treats providing they are not being used as a replacement for the essential foods from the five groups we have just looked at. In addition to excess sugar, salt should also be avoided when catering for children's diets. The kidneys of young children are not developed sufficiently to cope with high intakes of salt and it is important to bear in mind that some food stuffs already contain a high content of salt therefore children will receive sufficient salt for their necessary dietary intake without the need for adding more.

Finally, in addition to a healthy food intake, it is essential that childminders understand the importance of providing regular healthy drinks for children. The best options for drinks for children are milk or water. Water has been proven as being beneficial to brain development and it quenches thirst without interfering with appetite, unlike many other drinks. If you are considering providing bottled rather than tap water make sure that you opt for still and not carbonated or fizzy water. In addition to water, milk is an excellent alternative as it provides essential nutrients and calcium. Another reasonable option is unsweetened diluted fruit juice although these drinks should only be offered occasionally. Fizzy drinks should be avoided as much as possible as, in addition to curbing appetite and containing excessive amounts of sugar, they are also bad for children's teeth.

Exercise

Plan a weekly menu which will ensure that the children in your care are receiving the correct amount of healthy foods and drinks from each of the food groups listed previously.

Sensory development

Sensory development consists of the progress of the five senses which include:

- Sight
- Smell
- Touch
- Taste
- Sound

By using their senses babies and young children will gain information which allows them to make sense of their experiences. In the early years of a child's life the central nervous system which processes information relies heavily on the use of the senses to bring in information therefore a child with a sensory impairment may show some signs of delay in their overall development. Severe sensory impairments such as a total hearing or sight loss can be identified quickly however, it is important that childminders are aware of slight impairments which, although they will have an impact on the child's development, may be difficult to detect and therefore go unnoticed for some time.

We are surrounded by sensory experiences. Sensory experiences involve one or more of our five senses for example a restaurant would stimulate the following senses:

- Sight – people queuing for food or sitting eating, variety of foods on display attractively presented to look appetizing
- Smell – the smell of different foods being cooked
- Sound – the clatter of plates and cutlery, the sound of different voices engaged in conversation and the sounds from various machines such as coffee machines
- Taste – the taste of the food on offer

Children need to be allowed to explore in order to develop their own sensory awareness and they will rely heavily on the adults around them to help and encourage them to do so. Babies under the age of 12 months rely heavily on their sense of taste, touch and smell and they often demonstrate this by grasping objects and taking them to their mouths to investigate them. Older children will use all of their senses and each one will play an important part in their learning.

Exercise

Consider each of the five senses carefully and think about how you can help to stimulate the senses in both babies and older children. Look at the toys and resources you already offer and decide which ones encourage the use of certain senses. Can you add to your resources to successfully incorporate sensory development?

9 Creative Development

This chapter directly relates to

- Unit 2 of the Diploma in Home-based Childcare: Childcare and Child Development (0–16) in the Home-based Setting
- The Learning and Development Requirements of The Early Years Foundation Stage

Creativity means using the imagination to turn an idea into something creative. Creativity may take the form of painting a picture, making a house out of junk, baking a cake or making up a song. Young children will need adult support and encouragement in order to develop their creative flair as this does not come naturally and some children find being creative harder than others.

Being creative: responding to experiences, expressing and communicating ideas

Childminders can encourage the children in their care to be creative by developing their imagination and by providing props and resources in order for them to do this successfully.

Junk modelling, play dough, clay, baking, painting, drawing, sticking and gluing activities all encourage children to develop creativity and they should be provided regularly to the children in your care. It is best to avoid getting the children to copy something you have made yourself or furnishing them with colouring books, templates or stencils as these all limit the child's imagination and offer little or no opportunity for the child to develop their own ideas in order to produce something unique. Although children will enjoy colouring from pre-printed books, and these can be useful for children who find drawing difficult, they should only be offered occasionally so as to prevent curbing the child's own creative ideas. By developing ideas of their own, rather than following pre-set formulas, children can enjoy creating without fear of getting something wrong or producing a finished product that barely resembles what you intended it to be.

Exercise

Provide the children in your care with boxes, tubes, cartons and other items which can be used for junk modelling and let the children develop their own creations. Listen to what they are saying while they are working. How many times does the child change their mind about what they are making depending on how the product develops? Allowing a child to develop something which is unique to them, rather than asking them to copy something you have made or requesting that they produce something specific, allows their creativity to take over. Take note of how the children express and communicate their ideas among each other while they are being creative.

Being creative is all about exploring, experimenting and taking risks. Children should be allowed to experiment with a variety of tools in order to gain confidence when developing their creativity.

In the early stages of a child's development their creativity will be expressed through their desire to imitate the things around them. For example dressing up and role play is the obvious progression for a child who has watched their parents look after the house, go shopping and care for siblings. Dressing up and role play is something which both boys and girls will enjoy.

Small world toys begin to become interesting to a child once they reach the age of about 3 years. Small world toys are those which can be used to act out certain scenarios such as a train set, dolls house or farm. Older children may enjoy drama and dance as a way of realizing their creativity and they will begin to use these opportunities to explore their environment and personal experiences.

EXERCISE

Creativity opens up a huge world of opportunity for children. Make a list of all the toys, resources and games you can provide for the children in your care which will encourage their creative development.

Exploring media and materials

As previously mentioned children will imitate those around them and often the media influences the way in which a child will behave. Football heroes, pop stars and actors will all have some kind of an effect on impressionable young children who may try to emulate these celebrities. Unfortunately some children will be too young to understand that some of the behaviour is less desirable and should not be copied. Young children may wrongly assume that because famous people behave badly it is acceptable for them to copy this kind of behaviour. Childminders need to talk to the children and explain to them what kind of behaviour is and is not acceptable and role play is a good way of doing this successfully.

Exploring media and materials is a wonderful way of encouraging the creative development of children with respect to learning about cultures other than their own. Books, television, posters, etc. can all be used to reflect different home cultures and materials and props such as dressing up clothes, puppets, musical instruments etc. can be used to explore and experiment with in order to stimulate the children's imagination and interest.

Exploring music and dance

Most children will enjoy music and dance and they will happily sing along to their favourite tunes or make up dance moves without worrying about who is listening or watching. Young children are rarely self-conscious and as a result they tend to be able to express their feelings successfully in this way. Music can be enjoyed either by using commercially bought instruments or by making your own, and children should be encouraged to listen to a variety of different music ranging from loud to quiet and classical. Cultures can once again be explored with the use of music, and children should be encouraged to experiment with making different sounds and creating rhythm.

Exercise

Try putting a music CD on while the children are engrossed in play. What do the children do when the music plays? Observe even the youngest baby to see if they begin to move to the sounds.

Dance is a creative activity which children can use to stimulate both their imaginations and their bodies. By allowing children the opportunity to dance freely you will be encouraging them to explore their feelings through movement.

Developing imagination and imaginative play

Not all children find it easy to use their imagination and some will rely heavily on adult input in order for them to become engrossed in play. Imagination, like creativity, is impossible to teach in the way that you would teach scientific concepts. In order for children to become creative they need to develop their imagination. Creativity and imagination go hand in hand.

Babies use their imagination in the ways that they respond to people and their environment. They begin, at a very young age, to try to emulate the adults around them by copying facial expressions and movements. As the child gets older and their development progresses so too does their imagination and they begin to imitate the adults around them more and more often and in more complex ways such as copying their mother on the telephone, pretending to feed or bath a doll. Older children use role play, drama and dressing up to express their feelings and emotions.

Being able to play imaginatively means that children are able to create their own worlds in which to explore and express their feelings. Dressing up clothes and role play props are ideal for enhancing this type of play. In order to encourage a child to develop their imagination we must encourage them to rearrange their past experiences in a way that enables them to put ideas together in a new and interesting way.

Children are never too young to start developing their imagination and the most imaginative moments in a young child's life tend to occur spontaneously, although, having said this, it is still important for childcare practitioners to provide creative resources in order to develop these imaginative emotions and provide the child with an emotional outlet for their feelings. Imagination needs to develop freely and naturally and childminders have the difficult task of ensuring that the activities and resources they provide balance evenly and that they allow scope for the child to build on them and extend them suitably.

Imagination can be encouraged by allowing the children to take responsibility for as much of their creativity as possible. Avoid 'helping' a child to cut something out so that it appears

neatly trimmed, jagged edges may add to the overall effect and will make the finished product personal to the child. Allow the children the opportunity to choose their own materials and to explore freely as restricting their choices will control their imagination and limit their opportunity to be creative.

10 Promoting Children's Rights

This chapter directly relates to

- Unit 2 of the Diploma in Home-based Childcare: Childcare and Child Development (0–16) in the Home-based Setting
- The Welfare Requirements of The Early Years Foundation Stage

Childminders, along with parents, have a responsibility to protect the children in their care however, it is equally important that they understand the role they have in helping and encouraging children to become independent in order that they can be responsible for their own safety in time. Children cannot be under adult supervision all the time and, as they become older, they should be given more and more responsibility and freedom in order to allow them to gradually build on their independence and self-esteem. Competent childminders and parents recognize this and understand their role in helping children to gain the ability to understand that they will come across a variety of situations which they will need to understand and cope with as they grow and mature. It is therefore crucial for childminders to work with parents in order for them to build the child's confidence and self-esteem and to ensure that they are equipped with the necessary information vital to assist them in coping with unfamiliar situations.

The UN Convention on the Rights of the Child

The United Nations set out the basic rights of the child in 1959. These rights included providing a child with:

- Adequate nutrition
- Adequate housing
- Adequate medical care
- Free education
- The right to be allowed to play
- The right to be protected

In October 1991 the Children Act (1989) came into effect in the United Kingdom. This act spelt out how children should be cared for and stated that they have the right to be protected. The Act gave children certain rights and declared that they should be treated with respect. The Children Act had a huge impact on the role of the parents who, up until then, were viewed as having rights over their children. When the Children Act came into effect the emphasis was put on parents' *responsibility* for their children rather than their rights over them.

The Children Act specifically states that the child's best interests should be paramount at all times and also gives them rights to:

- Be protected.
- Have a chance to voice their opinions and preferences in any court cases which may involve them.
- Have access to their own solicitor.
- Have their wishes taken into account when any decisions about them are being made.
- Be kept informed of any decisions being made about them.
- Be kept informed of their rights.
- Be listened to.
- Be given the opportunity to air any worries they may have.
- Have their age, race, sex, culture, language and life experiences taken into account when any decisions are being made about them.
- Have the right to refuse a medical examination or assessment providing they understand what these involve.

In short, when the United Kingdom signed the UN Convention on the Rights of the Child in 1991, three main objectives were set out:

- The child's views
- Non-discrimination
- Best interests

The child's views

This right gives children the chance to voice their opinions and concerns and to say what they think about any issues which affect them.

Non-discrimination

This right ensures that all children are treated equally regardless of their race, religion, family background, sex, disability, language or life experiences.

Best interests

This right ensures that any decisions which are made by adults or organizations are done so with the best interests of the child at the forefront.

The historical and legislative background

If we take the time to think back to how children were regarded in the past we would see that they were treated in much the same way as adults. They were seen as being part of an adult society in most areas for example:

- They dressed in smaller versions of adult clothes.
- They worked alongside adults that is down the pits.
- They were punished for crimes in the same way as an adult; children could be sentenced to death or imprisonment.

Life was very difficult for children in the past with little means of escape or improvement. Education was seen in a completely different light than it is today and, instead of recognizing the significance of a decent education as being beneficial to the child, it was simply looked upon as being a way of providing the child with the skills needed for them to be useful in society when they were adults.

Things began to change in 1902 when The Education Act came into effect. This Act attempted to formalize education in Britain by introducing teachers. Finally, the introduction of The Children Act 1908 recognized children as being individuals. One of the significant outcomes of this Act was that no child under the age of 14 years could be sent to prison.

Save The Children was founded in 1919 by Eglantyne Jebb. In 1923 Jebb set out a summary of some of the essential rights of children and these were known as the Declaration of the Rights of the Child. The General Assembly of the International Save the Children Union agreed upon this declaration in 1923 and by 1924 the League of Nations had adopted it and it became known as the Declaration of Geneva. Although the declaration was not given any legally binding status it was a step in the right direction for a change in attitudes towards children.

There are a number of important pieces of legislation which have been brought into effect to recognize the rights of children and their families and these are set out below.

Sex Discrimination Act 1975: This Act was brought into effect to ensure that no individual is discriminated against because of their sex. The Act was supported by the Equal Opportunities Commission.

Race Relations Act 1976: This Act was amended in 2000 and states that equality of opportunity must be promoted and that all settings must have a suitable policy in place which is monitored and assessed.

Education Act 1981: This Act endorsed two major issues those of special educational needs and the rights of parents with regard to their children's education.

Education Reform Act 1988: The National Curriculum was introduced into schools.

United Nations Convention on the Rights of the Child 1989: This was a formal statement which was agreed upon by numerous nations. It states that all children have the right to adequate, decent food, adequate shelter and warmth, the right to education and the right to play.

Children Act 1989: 'The needs of the child are paramount', this was the phrase which summarized the Children Act 1989.

Education Act 1993: This Act gave parents the right to have their children, under the age of 2 years, to be formally assessed. The Act also brought about a code of practice for children with special educational needs.

Code of Practice for the Identification and Assessment of Children with Special Educational Needs 1994: This Code of Practice gave guidance on the responsibilities of the local education authorities and the governing bodies of schools to take into account children with special educational needs. The Code of Practice was revised in 2001.

Disability Discrimination Act 1995: This Act ensures that the rights of disabled people across England and Wales are met.

Education Act 1997: This Act encapsulated all Acts since 1944 and rolled them into one Act. It also set a time scale on the legal process for identifying a child's needs.

Data Protection Act 1998: This Act came into effect in order to prevent personal and confidential information being used without the person's consent. Consent for children must be issued by their parents.

National Standards for Under Eights Day Care and Childminding 2001: All registered childminders should be familiar with these 14 standards which were brought into effect so that Ofsted could monitor the way practitioners provide for children's rights, care and education.

Special Educational Needs and Disability Act 2001: This Act ensures that no child is discriminated against on the basis of their disability. It also ensures that settings make reasonable adjustments or alterations to their premises in order to accommodate the rights and needs of disabled children.

(Continued)

(Cont'd)

Birth to Three Matters 2002: A Framework for Effective Practice: This framework is not legislation however it was brought into effect to support, inform, guide and challenge childminders and all other early years childcare practitioners.

Children Act 2004: This Act came about from the Green Paper 'Every Child Matters' and is in place to identify the five outcomes which are considered essential for all children. These outcomes are to be healthy, to stay safe, to enjoy and achieve, to make a positive contribution and to achieve economic well-being.

Children Act 2006: This Act was intended to assist in the implementation of the aims set out in 'Choice for parents, the best start for children: a ten year strategy for children'.

Early Years Foundation Stage: A statutory framework for setting The Standards for Learning, Development and Care for Children from birth to five: The Early Years Foundation Stage is part of the ten-year childcare strategy 'Choice for parents, the best start for children' and the Children Act 2006. The EYFS has become a mandatory requirement for all schools and early years providers in Ofsted registered settings since September 2008. The EYFS principles are grouped into four distinctive themes and these are a unique child, positive relationships, enabling environments and learning and development.

The law and how it affects children and young people in the United Kingdom

The Children Act 1989 is one of the most important and influential laws protecting the rights of children and young people in the United Kingdom. It clearly states that children and their families need to have their rights protected and this is particularly important in cases such as divorce or formal separation when the welfare of the child, as well as that of the parents, needs to be considered. This means that when major decisions are being made such as who the child should reside with and where, children must be consulted, kept informed of any decisions and have their needs taken into consideration.

The Children Act 1989 also clearly states that children must not be prejudiced against regardless of their race, culture, language or religion and it is a legal requirement of all childcare practitioners, including childminders, to ensure that they treat all children in their care with equal concern at all times.

The rights of gay and lesbian people were recognized in 2005 and legislation which then came into effect now allows for same-sex civil partnerships which effectively gives gay and lesbian couples the same rights as heterosexual couples when it comes to issues such as pensions and benefits.

Inequality and the effects this has on children and their families

Despite all the laws and legislation which have come into effect the sad fact is that some children and their families still face discrimination. This may be for several reasons but is usually down to race, culture, religion or poverty.

Poverty is one of the biggest causes of inequality in the United Kingdom today. Living in poverty can have devastating results. A lack of money or transport may result in parents being unable to access quality childcare. The vicious cycle is reciprocated because, without quality childcare, parents are unable to move away from poverty and into paid employment or access suitable training.

Inequality has a negative effect on all children and their families. Labelling a person, pre-judging them and holding stereotypical opinions are all forms of prejudice and discrimination. One of the most detrimental, negative effects on children is the lack of self-esteem that prejudice inevitably brings about. A child who lacks self-esteem will be stripped of their identity, feel worthless and end up believing that the opinions others have of them are justified. The child will have problems forming friendships, feel a complete failure and be reluctant to rise or respond to challenges. All these feelings will bring about a feeling of inadequacy and eventually the child will come to expect that they are not worthy of success and accept what life throws at them without question.

It is the job of the childminder, along with the child's parents, to ensure that this does not happen to the children in their care. They have a responsibility to motivate the children, to promote positive images and to ensure that all children are treated with the respect they deserve. It has to be said however that not all discrimination is deliberate and sometimes we have to think very carefully, even when carrying out simple everyday tasks or activities, to make sure that we include all children. For example making a Mother's Day card may be appropriate for children who see their mother every day, but how would this make a child feel whose mother had died? Would it be appropriate for a child who lives with their father following the breakdown of their parents' relationship? Likewise not all children will celebrate Christian festivals and if you are used to getting children to make Christmas cards or decorate eggs for Easter you will need to make provision for children who do not celebrate these festivals in order to provide inclusion for *everyone* in your setting.

The way you respond towards people will have a huge impact on the children around you who often take their cue from adults they look up to and respect. It is therefore crucial that you ensure that your own reactions and responses are beyond reproach and that you make sure that you do not express any prejudice or stereotypical attitudes. Make sure that you answer any questions the children may have with open, honest information and encourage them to make enquiries about aspects they are unsure of as often ignorance is one of the main factors which lead to prejudice.

Children need to understand that people are all individuals, that we are all different with our own special traits. These differences, instead of resulting in prejudice and discrimination, should be embraced and seen as interesting. Never pretend that differences in people do not exist, offer explanations but never judgements.

Challenging discrimination and prejudice

It is not always easy to challenge discrimination and prejudice; however it is important that you ensure that the children in your care understand the need to treat people fairly and with respect. Some people shy away from challenging discrimination simply because this is the easiest solution and means that they do not have to tackle the issue. This is the wrong attitude to take because there are still many groups of people who are being penalized through discrimination and prejudice simply because some people are ignorant of the differences in others and think they have the right to cause distress.

Challenging discrimination is difficult and it takes a certain kind of resolve to ensure the desired outcome. The most important thing to remember is that discrimination and prejudice should never go ignored – everyone has a duty to challenge this kind of behaviour and stamp it out once and for all.

Children need to learn, from a young age, that showing prejudice and discrimination will not be tolerated and you may find some of the following strategies helpful when dealing with these kinds of issues:

- Always remember that children may not be aware that what they have said is hurtful or distressing. Tread carefully if you are confronting a child who has said something you consider to be offensive as they may not be completely aware that they have been disrespectful. Pay close attention to the fact that children often repeat things they have heard and that they may not completely understand what they have said. It is equally important however that you do not undermine something a child has repeated if they have heard their parents say it. It will be necessary, in these cases, to point out that prejudicial or discriminatory remarks will not be tolerated in your setting while at the same time explaining that everyone has the right to an opinion and that these opinions can differ considerably.
- Show care and understanding to any child who has borne the brunt of a hurtful or discriminatory remark. Comfort them and make sure that they understand that you do not share the same view and show them they are not treated differently in your setting and that they are welcome and valued.
- Always make sure that the children in your care understand your policy on discrimination and prejudice and that your rules are age appropriate. Children need to know that you will not tolerate anyone being excluded from games or activities.
- If you over hear a child making a hurtful remark always intervene. Explain why the remark is unacceptable and ensure that the child who made the remark is aware of the consequences of their actions and how a thoughtless comment can cause hurt and distress.

- Think about your own attitudes and the way you interpret things. For example, do you say fireman or policeman instead of officer, a description which successfully incorporates both genders? Do you consider dressing up and playing with dolls to be for girls? Are all boys expected to take part in rough and tumble games or sporting events in your setting?
- Finally, be brave! There may come a time when you will need to challenge a parent rather than a child who makes a discriminatory or prejudicial remark in your setting and, once again, you should not ignore or shy away from your responsibilities. Politely point out that you do not share their opinion and refer the parent to your equal opportunities policy. You may embarrass the parent or even make them angry however one thing is for sure you will prompt them to think about their remarks and hopefully curb their opinions in the future!

Exercise

Spend some time thinking about how you would deal with the statements outlined below. Would you challenge the person making the remarks or would you ignore what has been said?

- 'Boys will be boys' a comment made by the father of a child who has just pushed another child to the ground.
- 'We only eat English food at our house, please don't feed foreign food to Melissa it upsets her digestive system' a comment made by a parent to a childminder who has served Spaghetti Bolognese for lunch.
- 'She is such a pretty girl, it is a shame she has such a terrible lisp' comments overheard in the playground between two parents.

11 Working with Disabled Children and Their Families

This chapter directly relates to

- Unit 2 of the Diploma in Home-based Childcare: Childcare and Child Development (0–16) in the Home-based Setting
- Unit 5 of the Diploma in Home-based Childcare: Planning to Meet Children's Individual Learning Needs in the Home-based Setting
- The Learning and Development Requirements of The Early Years Foundation Stage

More and more parents of children with disabilities are turning to childminders for childcare as they see home-based carers as being more in tune with the additional needs their child may require. They like the home from home environment and feel that their children are more able to cope away from the family setting if they spend time in a similar environment with one carer rather than in a purpose built nursery setting catering for large numbers of children and with different members of staff caring for them.

A disability need not necessarily be very severe and it is estimated that up to a fifth of all children in the United Kingdom have some kind of disability or impairment therefore, although working with disabled children brings with it different challenges and issues, it is also a worthwhile venture which all childminders would do well to consider.

Understanding disabilities in children

Finding the right childcare is a daunting issue for all working parents; however the problems and stresses are increased dramatically when the child in question has a disability. Parents will worry whether their child is in the right kind of environment, whether they are included in all the activities or whether they are facing discrimination and it is the job of the child-minder to ensure that any worries or fears they may have are put to rest.

It is vital that childminders treat all children as individuals and that they encourage others in their setting to do the same in order to avoid discrimination or prejudice. A child should never be labelled because of their impairment or medical condition and they need to be accepted for who they are not what they look like or what condition they may have. It is important to think carefully about how you describe people and whether or not you unintentionally 'label' people in order to set a good example for the children in your care to follow. For example have you ever referred to someone as 'the lady with the glasses' or 'the child with the limp/stutter etc.' Do you see twins as individuals in their own right with their own identity, or do you couple them together giving them a label?

Exercise

Take some time to consider the 'labels' which have been used to describe disabled people. How would you respond if you overheard someone describing a disabled person as being a 'cripple', 'spastic' or 'retard'?

It is not always easy to define children with a disability. This is because, although children with disabilities share the same basic needs as other children, their disability may affect how these needs are met or create additional needs. The one thing which does define a child with special needs is that they will need *additional* help in some areas of development when compared with other children. It is crucial that childminders look first and foremost at the *child as an individual* and only then should they consider any special needs.

Everyone has their own individual strengths and weaknesses. Each individual will show a different pattern of behaviour and development and each will have their own opinions, values and attitudes. Children with a disability are no exception and although they need their disability to be recognized and understood this is not the same as having them labelled, pitied or made to feel inferior.

Definitions of impairment and disability

Understanding disabilities in children is very important and crucial to the role of a child-minder. Disability, impairment and difficulty are three very separate conditions and we need to fully understand the differences in each.

- **Disability** – this is when someone experiences a mental or physical condition which affects their movements or senses. Cerebral Palsy, which affects one in every 400 children born in the United Kingdom, for example limits mobility and is classed as a disability so too are conditions such as Cystic Fibrosis and Downs Syndrome.
- **Impairment** – this is a condition which affects a person's ability to see, hear, walk or coordinate their actions effectively.
- **Difficulty** – although some difficulties, such as emotional problems, can be overcome others, which may affect behaviour for example ADHD, may be much harder to keep under control.

Some of the essential skills necessary to make a good childminder are:

- A sense of humour
- A calm and patient disposition
- A fair and consistent approach to managing behaviour

However, when caring for children with a disability it is necessary for the individual to possess a number of other, essential skills such as:

- Physical fitness – you may have to lift a child.
- Willingness to undertake essential training.
- Competence in using necessary aids and administering regular medication.
- Willingness to source additional information and advice when necessary.
- Optimism.
- Being realistic.
- Competence in carrying out therapy if necessary.

Inclusion of children with disabilities

Children with a disability are much the same as any other child in that they need to have friends, feel safe both physically and emotionally and feel that they belong. All children, regardless of their ability, should be encouraged to live up to their full potential. They should be provided with the necessary resources and experiences in order to explore and work things out for themselves and every child should be celebrated for his or her uniqueness.

There may be times, when caring for a child with a disability, when it is necessary to call upon the professional services of doctors, therapists, health visitors etc., and it is important for childminders to work closely with the child's parents in cases such as these in order to provide the best possible care for the child. The list below gives some of the services you may like to contact with regard to sourcing help, with parental permission, when caring for disabled children:

- Doctors
- Health visitors
- Speech therapists
- Physiotherapists
- Home learning schemes that is Portage, a scheme designed to provide trained visitors to work with young children and their parents in the home
- Toy libraries – useful for borrowing items of equipment and toys which have been specially adapted for disabled children

Although sometimes it can be difficult to make sure that you include all the children in your care in every activity and experience it is absolutely essential that you think about the areas a disabled child will need additional help in and ensure that you provide this in order to fully include them in the setting.

In order to include *all* children you will need to consider:

Children with physical disabilities

These children may have problems with gross motor skills. They may find it difficult to maintain balance and they may frequently stumble or fall. They may lack the skill to walk, run, jump or climb and, if they are able to do some of these, their mobility may be very limited. They may be unable to catch or throw a ball. A child who experiences problems with fine motor skills may be unable to grasp or hold things effectively and they may have poor hand/eye coordination.

In order to provide inclusion for a child with a physical disability it may be necessary for you to consider:

- Providing lots of soft furniture and equipment to reduce the risk of injury if the child should fall against it.
- Providing stable, heavy furniture which will not be knocked over easily should the child fall against it.
- Ensuring that doors are wide enough and that door handles and light switches are easily accessible.
- Ensuring that your furniture and equipment is arranged in a sensible manner so that a child in a wheel-chair for example has ample space to manoeuvre and can easily access toys and resources.
- Providing suitable storage for special equipment such as walking sticks, callipers etc. to ensure that they do not pose a risk to other children in the setting.
- Providing suitable toys, resources and equipment. For example think about fixing bowls to the table with tape or purchasing suction bowls and plates to assist children when feeding, baking etc. Consider how you can make all the children comfortable and provide bean bags if necessary. Talk to the child's parents to find out the best solution to making the child comfortable.

Children with hearing impairments

A child who is deaf or has a hearing impairment may not respond when they are spoken to. They may rarely speak and when they do speak this could be in either a very loud or a very soft voice and they may be difficult or even impossible to understand. A child with a hearing impairment may find it difficult to understand or follow verbal direction and may often interrupt conversations or appear unaware that others are speaking.

In order to provide inclusion for a child with hearing impairments it may be necessary for you to consider:

- Making eye contact with the child before you speak so that they are aware that you are talking to them.
- Learning how to use sign language and appropriate facial expressions and hand gestures.
- Ensuring that your setting has lots of visual cues for example toy boxes that are clearly labelled with a picture of the contents attached so that the child can see immediately what is inside which will help them to take part in self-selecting toys and tidying away activities.
- Making sure that all background noise in the setting is kept to a minimum to make it easier for the child to concentrate on what is being said.

Children with visual impairments

Children with visual impairments usually have some kind of vision, and a person who is considered totally blind can often differentiate light from dark. It goes without saying that a child with a visual impairment will often be delayed in other areas of their development such as gross and fine motor skills. This may be down to being unable to locate small objects or being afraid to explore and investigate space for fear or injury or failure.

In order to provide inclusion for a child with visual impairments it may be necessary for you to consider:

- Reviewing your lighting to ensure that it is adequate and that all rooms are lit to the same degree. Sometimes moving from a brightly lit room to a dull one and vice versa can have a negative impact on a child with a visual impairment.
- Arranging your furniture to ensure that there is plenty of space for the child to move around safely and that clutter is kept to a minimum. Avoid changing the room layouts so that the child can become comfortable knowing where everything is in the setting. Being confident that they can locate their favourite toys and equipment will enhance their self-esteem.
- Providing lots of soft furniture to avoid injury if the child bangs into it. Avoid sharp corners, rugs etc.
- Providing lots of sensory experiences, toys and resources.

Providing play and learning activities for disabled children

All children need adults around them who will encourage play and learning activities rather than direct them. Children with a disability are no different in their needs than other children.

In the same way as able-bodied children a disabled child needs to be able to express themselves freely and take part in age-appropriate activities and experiences which challenge, excite and interest them.

One of the most important considerations a childminder will need to take into account when caring for a disabled child and providing for their play and learning activities is to *never make assumptions!* It should not be assumed that a child who wears a leg calliper cannot climb or that a child in a wheelchair will not enjoy feeling the sand between their toes. It may be necessary for you to adapt some of your toys and equipment and you may have to allow extra time for certain activities however it is absolutely crucial that you do not discriminate against a child with disabilities because you *assume* they cannot do something or will not enjoy it as a result of their disability. Often the stumbling block, when caring for disabled children, is not the fact that the equipment or resources are unsuitable and need adapting, more commonly it is the childminder's approach to play and activities which needs rethinking.

Planning is important when caring for all children in order to ensure that their needs are met however, when caring for disabled children, effective planning is absolutely crucial. Consider which activities you are intending to offer the children and think about ways you can adapt these activities to include disabled children. A child who has difficulty with hand–eye coordination for example may find painting difficult however with your help to guide their hands and a selection of suitable painting materials such as stamps, chunky brushes, rollers etc. this activity can be easily adapted to include all the children. Resist limiting your ideas and explore as many possibilities as you can. Who says painting activities need to involve brushes?

When planning your activities take the opinions of the children into account. Ask the children what they would like to do and, if they come up with something which you think is unsuitable for a disabled child explain this clearly and invite suggestions from everyone as to how the requested activity can be suitably adapted to include everyone.

Make sure that your toys, equipment and activities are easily accessible to everyone and position things so that all children can select what they wish to play with independently.

It is a good idea for childminders, who are caring for a child with a disability, to put themselves in the child's shoes. Look around your setting and ask yourself some questions and, more importantly, answer them truthfully. If you were a child in a wheelchair would you feel welcome and comfortable in the setting? Could you access all the toys and equipment easily or would you need to ask for assistance? Would you feel included in all the planned activities and outings? What would you like to see changed or improved? When you have answered these questions truthfully, use your findings to rethink your planned activities and the layout of your setting so that they are better suited to provide for total inclusion.

There are a number of outlets where specially adapted toys and resources can be purchased for disabled children however these often prove very expensive. You may like to use the facilities of your local toy library to source suitable toys or to glean ideas of how best to adapt or improve upon your existing equipment.

Working with families of disabled children

One of the most important aspects of a childminder's job is to understand the importance of the parents' role in caring for their child. Parents are the most knowledgeable people in their child's life and as such they need to be consulted in all aspects of their child's care. A relationship with parents based on mutual understanding and respect is absolutely crucial for all childminders however, for those providing care for disabled children, the relationship you have with the parents may be even more important as you will often have to work together to provide support and to share anxieties or concerns.

It is important that childminders not only understand the child well and are aware of their disability and what it involves, it is also crucial that they realize that the child's disability may have had a huge, and often devastating, impact on the whole family.

Parents who have been informed of a disability in their child may experience some or all of the following emotions:

- Guilt – this may be aimed towards themselves or their partner.
- Blame – once again this may be aimed towards themselves or their partner and may even be extended to medical professionals.
- Shock – being unable to take in what is happening.
- Anger – that this is happening to their child.
- Desperation – feeling unable to cope and not knowing where to turn for help.
- Grief – feeling a sense of loss for what could have been, and having their expectations for their child suddenly shattered.
- Fear – worrying what the future holds for their child.
- Stress – endless hospital visits, physiotherapy, medication etc. can have a devastating effect on family life. Financial problems due to the expense of having to provide special equipment or adapting the house can also add to stress.
- Shame – the attitudes of friends, neighbours, work colleagues and even family can have a devastating effect on the family.
- Rejection – some parents find it very difficult to accept their child's disability and may end up rejecting the child completely.
- Denial and disbelief – this is often experienced by parents who are unable to cope or who secretly blame themselves for their child's condition.

Once these emotions have been confronted and the situation looked at rationally many parents cope admirably, however in some circumstances parents are unable to work together and end up separating. The end of any relationship brings with it untold misery and uncertainty, couple this with caring for a disabled child, and it is easy to see why parents need understanding and support.

In order to provide support for the parents, make sure that you have the time to listen to them sympathetically and be interested in what they have to tell you. Try to gather as much information as you can about their child's disability and share this information with the child's parents so that they understand that you are genuinely interested in their child and are willing to help them as much as you can. Rarely are parents praised for the marvellous job they do and often this is all that is needed to encourage a parent who is feeling a little down and to boost their confidence.

It is important that childminders focus on the social model of disability, that is acknowledging those with a disability as being first and foremost a person in their own right, rather than the medical model, that is seeing only the problems of the persons disability, in order to help parents to keep their negative feelings in check and focus on the positive aspects of bringing up their child so that they can take pleasure in their child's achievements and support them in their development.

Always include parents of disabled children in the work that you do and share with them their child's achievements, however small. Keep parents informed of their child's progress and involve them every step of the way so that they do not feel different or isolated from the other families whose children you are caring for.

Each family will be unique in the way that they adjust to caring for a disabled child. Having a disabled child will affect the whole family and the way that it operates including social, financial and psychological consequences.

It is important to remember that families with a child who has a disability have particular needs of their own that arise from a demanding caring role. Although the family may have additional help caring for their child in the form of respite care or holiday play schemes, there will still be times when everything becomes too much for them and the stress and anxiety brought about caring round the clock for a disabled child can be overwhelming. Try to be there for them when needed and offer help and support or even just listen to them and provide a shoulder to cry on when things threaten to engulf them.

Try to get as much information about the child's disability as possible and ask parents for help and advice. Although medical information is vital when caring for a child with a disability it is equally important to remember to look at the child as a whole, to see past their disability and treat them as an individual who has an important contribution to make to the childcare setting.

Exercise

Spend some time investigating the services provided by your own local authority and the voluntary organizations in your area which may be able to provide information and resources for children with special needs.

12 Working in Partnership with Parents

This chapter directly relates to

- Unit 2 of the Diploma in Home-based Childcare: Childcare and Child Development (0–16) in the Home-based Setting
- Unit 4 of the Diploma in Home-based Childcare: Working in Partnership with Parents in the Home-based Setting
- The Welfare Requirements of The Early Years Foundation Stage

It is absolutely paramount that childcare practitioners work in partnership with the parents of the children placed in their care to ensure a good working relationship which is beneficial to everyone concerned. Practitioners need to take the time to talk to the child's parents to ascertain a suitable strategy for caring for their child and to ensure continuity of care. Practitioners and parents need to communicate *regularly* and *effectively* in order to establish a good rapport so that the parents can be confident that their chosen childcare practitioner is right for them and, more importantly, for their child.

Types of families

Whatever kind of family setup a child comes from you must always remember that the child's parents are the most knowledgeable people when it comes to their children. They will have intimate knowledge and understanding of their child – and, as such, they should be treated with respect. Most parents want the best for their children however, types of family setups can differ enormously and these will have an effect on parenting styles and subsequently how the child is brought up. You may not always agree with or understand a particular family setup however, it is crucial that you accept the differences in family types and treat each with the respect they deserve.

The main types of family setups are as follows:

- **The nuclear family** – this is where a child lives with both their natural mother and father and the parenting responsibilities are shared equally between them.
- **The extended family** – this is where parents, children and relatives all live in close proximity to each other, sometimes even in the same house, and share the responsibility for bringing up the children. This type of family setup was very common in the United Kingdom for centuries and it is still widely practised in many parts of the world today.
- **The single-parent family** – this is where the child lives with just one parent. Single-parent families can come about for a number of reasons: one parent may have died, the mother and father of the child may have separated or divorced or the mother may have actively chosen to have a child alone without support from the father.
- **The reconstituted family** – this kind of family setup is very common today with an increase in divorce. Reconstituted families come about when one natural parent and one step-parent live together with the children.
- **The adoptive family** – this is where a child is not living with either of their natural parents. In some cases the child may not be aware that they are adopted and may therefore believe they are living in a nuclear family.

In addition to family structures, parenting styles also need to be taken into consideration when working in partnership with parents. There may well be situations which arise where you do not completely agree with the way a parent handles a situation or chooses to discipline their child and it is important to understand the different parenting styles in order to work effectively with parents. For example an over-domineering parent, who tries to control their child, may be completely at odds with your own ideas, opinions and policies and, likewise a parent who allows their child untold freedom and fails to show their child any boundaries at all may also prove difficult for you to work with. In order to strike up an effective working relationship with parents it is essential, first and foremost, that you understand and accept the differences in family setups and parenting styles, only then can you begin to work together. Remember there is no right or wrong way of bringing up a child and what may work well for one family could be completely unacceptable to another. Although you will need to tread carefully if your own views and opinions differ considerably from the parents of the children you are caring for, it is still possible for you to provide an effective childcare service and to work in partnership with the parents based on mutual respect and understanding.

Generally speaking parents fall into one of the following three groups:

- **Authoritarian** – this parent tries to control their child. They will have lots of rules in a bid to try to manage their child's behaviour and their expectations of what is and is not acceptable will be very high often resulting in a child who underachieves by failing to reach their parent's exceptionally high expectations, leaving them feeling undervalued and lacking in confidence.
- **Permissive** – this parent is the total opposite of an authoritarian one. They will allow their child total control and freedom of choice which will often result in the child being difficult to manage in respect of their behaviour as they are unaware of the need for suitable boundaries. Permissive parents may produce children who are afraid to try things out or make choices for fear of making mistakes.
- **Authoritative** – this is the happy medium style of parenting which most mothers and fathers fall into. This type of parent strives to ensure that their child will be accepted in society by providing them with a reasonable set of rules in which to live by.

Communication between childminders, parents and school

Ideally childminders and parents will take the time to speak to one another on a daily basis, either when the child is being dropped off at the childminder's home or when they are being collected. However, this is not always possible and often, due to the stress of busy working lives and long working hours, parents and childminders may become complacent when it comes to communication. However, in order for the childminder to provide the best quality childcare it is necessary for everyone to make the time to discuss the child's care *regularly*. If this cannot be done on a daily basis then it is essential that time is put aside, perhaps once a week, to talk things through, iron out any concerns or problems or simply discuss the child's progress. It may be necessary for the childminder and parent to arrange time out of working hours, perhaps over a cup of coffee, when no one is in a rush to get to work and the pace is less hectic.

Any minor concerns, if left unchecked, can quickly escalate and end up becoming huge problems if they are not discussed at the very outset and often the longer a problem is left to fester, the more difficult it is to raise the issue and for this reason alone childminders and parents must work together in order to forge a good working relationship.

Childminders, like all adults, are not mind readers and we cannot forsee problems or anticipate situations and sometimes things may need to be pointed out. If a childminder, or indeed a parent, appears to be expecting something over and above what has been agreed or if the initial childcare arrangements appear to be inadequate, over a period of time, then the arrangements must be discussed and an alternative solution sought before relations break down irreparably.

Often childminders will take children to and collect them from playgroup, nursery and school and it may be that the child's parents rarely, if ever, venture into the school environment. For this reason it is essential that childminders work closely with the child and their parents to ensure that they are kept up to date with what is going on within the school premises and the childminder will need to liaise between the parents and school regularly. Parents can often feel quite alienated by their child's school life if they never get a chance to go into school, meet the teacher etc., and they may feel that they are missing out on this aspect of their child's life. By working closely together with the school, on behalf of the parents, you can help to bridge the gap. Young children are not always proficient in remembering things and it may be necessary for you to liaise with the school, on behalf of the child and their parents in ways such as:

- Ensuring that lunch money is handed in.
- Ensuring that homework is handed in *on time*.
- Making sure that children remember to bring home important letters and that these are given to the parents and not left in the child's school bag.
- Keeping the parents informed of all school holidays, training days etc.
- Keeping the parents informed of clubs run by the school such as sports or dancing classes.
- Ensuring that parents are aware of any homework the child is expected to do and whether they have done it with you or not.
- Ensuring that parents are aware of any celebrations, concerts etc. the school is taking part in.

Some parents will request that their child does homework they have been set at your house; others will prefer them to do it at home where they can participate. This is of course all a matter of preference and a lot will depend on the number of hours the child spends with you compared to how long they will have at home and what other things the parents have planned. Problems can arise however if a child refuses to do their homework with you despite their parent requesting it. They may be tired after spending long hours at school and simply wish to wind down and enjoy playing games with their friends and resent having to do more school work as soon as they get to your house. Talk to the child's parents if you are faced with this kind of problem and offer suggestions or alternatives. You may like to suggest:

- That the child shares their homework between the setting and home. For example homework on Monday, Tuesday and Wednesday could be carried out at home while homework set on Thursday and Friday could be done in the childcare setting.
- Arrange a special treat, with the parent's consent, as an incentive when the homework is completed.
- Allow the child time to wind down and play when they get back to the setting before encouraging them to tackle their homework, practise their spellings or read to you.

Always make sure that parents are aware that you will not force their child into doing their homework at your house and that they must talk to their child and explain what they would like to happen so that you do not feel like the villain responsible for making sure that homework gets done. While it is important that you work with the parents in situations such as these it is equally important that parents understand that it is not your responsibility to get their child to do their homework if they flatly refuse.

Whenever possible try to go into school and look around the child's class. Take note of the work they are doing during each particular term – often schools send home letters informing parents of the themes and topics the children will be studying that term – and you would be advised to read these. It is also important to talk to the children themselves and encourage them to tell you what is going on in school, what they are learning etc. and you should then try to extend what the child is learning in school in your own setting, without boring them. Avoid repetition but think of ways you can continue any themes from school with the work that you do with the children to highlight and increase their knowledge and information.

Working together to provide for children's development and well-being

In all aspects of the work you do as a childminder it is important that you understand the need to work in partnership with the child's parents. However, you also need to understand the importance of ensuring that the welfare of the child is paramount. It will be necessary for you to show that you are a reflective practitioner and that you are able to successfully evaluate your own practice and attitudes while taking into account the preferences and wishes of parents and understand the central role that parents play in the life of their child.

In order for you to work with parents to benefit the children's development and well-being you will need to understand your own limits and be aware of where the boundaries of your responsibilities lie. It may, at times, be necessary for you to point parents in the direction of professional help and advice and you should never be afraid to say if you are unsure of something if a parent asks for your advice. Use your professional judgement to decide when you can help parents and when, what they may be asking of you is beyond your limitations.

Establishing and maintaining a good relationship with parents is the key to running a successful childminding business and providing for children's development and well-being. Having the parents on your side and knowing that what you are doing is being reciprocated in the home environment is absolutely essential. Children will feel secure and valued when they are aware of the boundaries and they will be happy in the knowledge that their parents and childminder like and respect one another. You do not need to be bosom buddies with all the parents of the children in your setting in order to establish a successful working relationship, it is sufficient that you both understand what it is that each of you are trying to achieve in respect of the development and well-being of the children.

In order to work together effectively you may like to:

- Ask parents for their opinions on a regular basis and, more importantly, *listen* to what they say and take their comments and suggestions on board.
- Try to involve the children's families in your planned activities or themes. For example if you care for a child from an ethnic background perhaps you could invite a parent or grandparent in to talk

about their religion or enlist their help making different foods – children often love having visitors to talk to and the child whose grandparent/parent has agreed to help will feel extra special and valued.

- Create a notice board in your setting so that parents can access relevant information.
- Involve parents in all aspects of their child's care and exchange information with them on a regular basis.

Continuity of care is vital for the development and well-being of children and it is crucial that you work well with the child's parents at all times. Conflict should be avoided at all costs as children are very adept at picking up on tension and their development and well-being can be adversely affected if their parents and childminder appear at loggerheads. Always communicate with parents in a respectful manner and work through any problems immediately so that an amicable solution can be found without any repercussions on the child's care.

Exercise

Think about your own relationships with the parents of the children in your care. Do you get on better with some parents than others? Does the way you relate to the child's parents have any effect on your relationship with the child? Why do you think it is important not to have 'favourites' when it comes to parents and their children? How do you think you can improve a relationship with a parent if you consider it to be inadequate?

List of Useful Addresses

www.childgrowthfoundation.org
Child Growth Foundation
2 Mayfield Avenue, Chiswick, London, W4 1PW
Telephone 020 8995 0257

www.ncb.org.uk
Council for Disabled Children
Wakley Street, London, EC1V 7QE
Telephone 020 7843 6061

www.home-start.org.uk
Home-Start UK
2 Salisbury Road, Leicester, LE1 7QR
Telephone 0116 233 9955
This organization offers support and practical advice to families with children under the age of 5 years
of age who are experiencing difficulties.

www.ican.org.uk
I CAN
8 Wakley Street, London, EC1V 7QE
Telephone 0845 225 4071
This organization offers support for children with communication disabilities.

www.kids.org.uk
KIDS
6 Aztec Row, Berners Road, London, N1 0PW
Telephone 020 7359 3635
This organization offers support for disabled children.

www.ndcs.org.uk
National Deaf Children's Society (NDCS)
15 Dufferin Street, London, EC1Y 8UR
Telephone 020 7490 8656

www.reach.org.uk
REACH
PO Box 54, Helston, Cornwall, TR13 8WD
Telephone 0845 1306 2251
This organization offers support for children with hand or arm deficiency.

ww.rnib.org.uk
Royal National Institute for the Blind (RNIB)
105 Judd Street, London, WC1H 9NE
Telephone 020 7388 1266

www.sebda.org
SEBDA
Room 211, The Triangle, Exchange Square, Manchester, M4 3TR
Telephone 0161 240 2418
This organization offers support for children experiencing difficulties in their social, emotional and behavioural development.

Index